Philosophy's Own Religion

Don Cupitt

Philosophy's Own Religion

scm press

0 334 02811 6

First published 2000
by SCM Press
9–17 St Albans Place, London N1 0NX

SCM Press is a division of
SCM-Canterbury Press Ltd

Typeset by Regent Typesetting, London
and printed in Great Britain by
Biddles Ltd, Guildford and King's Lynn

Contents

Preface

In this book I attempt to describe the philosophy and the religion of the future. In Part One, Fore Words, there are some necessary preliminaries about what the philosophy of religion has been hitherto, and why it is now changing so rapidly. In Part Two, We and Our World, I outline the way our philosophical situation now looks, as I have done – in somewhat different terms – two or three times before. I have earlier called it 'the last philosophy',[1] meaning that it is what we come to 'at the end of history', when we have given up the illusions, the pedagogical fictions and the elements of ideology that were present in the philosophy of the past, and when we have given up every sort of belief that subordinates this world to a greater and better world, either above, or yet to come. Now, we see this world as 'the world at the end of the world', and as being simply and outsidelessly *our* world. I have also called the situation described here 'language's own philosophy',[2] meaning that, as the human communication-system, language must seek to construct reality as a network of speakers and hearers set in a humanly appropriated world, the whole being posited by, held within, and sustained by the endless flow of communication, pouring out and passing away. The world that talk builds has to be a radical-humanist world, and a world that is made of and held within language.

I am saying, then, that the philosophy here described represents where philosophy by its own logic must end. Personally, I think we are already there, but you may if you prefer picture us as being still a little short of the final destination.

Then in Part Three, The Teaching, we turn to religion. Because we now see (or are fast coming to see) our world as being the last

world and the only world, we do not need any beliefs about
another world, and our religion will be dogmaless. This is something of a relief, because it is now apparent that there are no
strictly, or 'dogmatically', true religious beliefs. Instead, we face
the novel and interesting task of giving a clear and organized
account of purely this-worldly and non-dogmatic religious existence. How is one to write the systematic theology of beliefless
religion? It is not easy, because westerners have such a strong
propensity to equate faith with creed, and religion with the
holding of supernatural beliefs. They find it hard to accept that
beliefless religion can be interesting, or even that it makes any
sense; but then, it is also hard to accept that the old western
cultural epoch dominated in philosophy by the Greeks, and in
religion by Christian ecclesiastical theology, has now come to an
end.

However, it has now ended, after two millennia. Until about
1990 I believed and hoped that church reform was possible,
provided that one were allowed to interpret traditional belief in
a non-realistic way (1980–85), or provided that the church's
disciplinary control of truth were relaxed enough to permit a
decentred, 'disseminated', much more fluid and plural, motion of
religious symbols (1986–89). During the early 1990s, however,
and amid much turmoil, I had to admit the vanity of such hopes.
Most people could not understand the 'non-realist' and action-
guiding or 'regulative' interpretation of traditional doctrine, and
would not accept that until the thirteenth century something very
close to it, the 'negative theology', had been regarded as orthodox. Like an earlier philosophical theologian with similar
views, H. L. Mansel (1820–71), I was taken to be propagating
'atheism'. It was clear that I could get nowhere, and this present
book marks a break with 'Christian non-realism' as a proposal
to reform and renew ecclesiastical Christianity by changing the
way people understand their own religious beliefs. Despite the
church's precipitate decline, reform is clearly not on the agenda.

The present book, then, presents a summary of my own final
outlook. It is not addressed to the church. I am trying to get it as
near right as it can be got, just for me and for others who think

as I do. This is not 'Christian non-realism' any longer, but an attempt to state briefly the last philosophy and the last form of religion, after Plato and after the church. During the 1990s and in spite of it all I did produce a dozen books that can be referred to by anyone who looks for more detail and more supporting arguments, in order to put flesh on the skeleton presented here. It will be noticed that although my outlook is becoming post-ecclesiastical, it is not as post-Christian as it seemed to be a few years ago. In fact, I seem to find ways of salvaging a good deal of Christian religion, despite having dispensed with Christian doctrinal beliefs. The reason for this is that after the church has completed its historical task it is followed, not by an irreligious age, but by an age of religious fulfilment. In the ecclesiastical period religion is mediated by doctrinal beliefs held upon authority, but in the 'kingdom' period that follows religion becomes immediate and beliefless.

For many years I have had a habit of coining brief slogans, and two of them should be mentioned here at the very beginning. The first is the phrase 'democratic philosophy'. Historically, philosophy was an élite subject. People proficient in it had become very different from the common run of humanity, and deserved to rule society. But, for obvious reasons, that conception of philosophy is inappropriate now. If philosophy is to be of use in a democratic age, it must be written in a generally accessible style and must be fully up-to-date. In addition, it needs to pay close attention to the way words move in ordinary language.

I am, then, trying to present avant-garde ideas in philosophy and religion in as democratic a style as I can muster. The second slogan is 'there is no correct terminology'. In traditional religion there is an idea that you must use exactly the right names for your gods, and exactly the right words when pronouncing spells or administering sacraments. In Christianity these ideas were taken to an extreme as dogma was defined; religious language came to be policed very strictly, and suspected heretics found their writings undergoing minute scrutiny. Spreading into philosophy, the same mentality came to examine texts very closely to determine exactly in what sense words were being used and what doctrines were being taught. Much philosophy came to be written on the assumption that a super-precise use of language that gets it exactly right is possible, is desirable and is even compulsory. Language is seen as being used, before all else, to state one's precise doctrinal position.

I want to reject that whole tradition, because it ends in sterile scholasticism. Philosophical writing should not aim to get it exactly right in a lawyer's sense, but it can hope from time to time to get something right in the way that poetry can. The way that poetry can do what? Can . . . hit it off, is the phrase.[3] But, like poets, we should avoid getting ourselves locked into any standard terminology. Compulsory stock phrases, used as passwords, kill thought.

Some clichés, however, are difficult to avoid. A recent exhibition[4] has reminded us that popular post-modern religious art is, precisely, kitsch – the kitsch portrayal of Diana, Princess of Wales, as the Virgin Mary and of Leonardo DiCaprio as Saint Sebastian. So, I ask myself, how can I avoid the obvious corollary that my democratic religious philosophy must turn out to be, precisely, kitsch philosophy, trading in all the banal platitudes about 'life' that real philosophers take care to avoid like the plague? I am embarrassed by this thought and do not know how to escape the difficulty, except by invoking the way the young Wordsworth somehow manages to get away with dropping the usual poetic diction and embracing ordinary language. We live in a time when a move of that kind urgently needs to be made, both in philosophy and in religion. I can further adduce in my defence the argument put forward in the 'Everyday Speech' books, namely that the popular philosophy and the religious thought that are embedded in ordinary language are not in fact as 'low' and 'banal' as has traditionally been supposed. A democratic approach to philosophy must and will take ordinary language seriously – as I do again here, when I cite relevant phrases from ordinary language.

My philosophy of religion, then, takes the form of an attempt to describe how things look at the end of the line, where we come to the last philosophy and, corresponding to it, the last form of religion; both being populist or democratic. Roughly, we are talking about democratic and ordinary-language philosophy, and about 'kingdom' religion. But I am still not presenting a large-scale systematic work, which will disappoint one recent commentator, who complains that my books 'seem more akin to work in progress than to substantial summas'.[5] My reply to this complaint is that for me, as for Nietzsche, Bultmann and many others, there is no realm of unchanging and objective truth for a systematic philosophy or a systematic theology to be *about*. Reality has no permanent intelligible structure of its own: everything is humanly projected, changing and contingent. Religion is now perforce about learning to love uncertainty, secondariness and transience, and the only *summa* I can offer is the linear series of my books and the fidelity (or otherwise) of their witness to the way the human situation has been changing in my time. The twentieth century was described early on as 'the century of the common man', and it was perhaps inevitable that at its end I should feel that the end of the story (or maybe it's only the end of my story) is the return into ordinariness. This theme, that the last word lies with ordinary life, resounded through the century from Tolstoy at its beginning, through Wittgenstein in its middle years, and on to Stanley Cavell and various others of us at its close.

A last point: by introducing slogans such as 'language's own philosophy' and 'philosophy's own religion' in this book I am hinting at a new approach to an old question, the question of metaphysics. Everyone who thinks has at one time or another wondered how we can ever get into the right position, find the right method and the right vocabulary, for dealing with the questions of how we come to be here, what we are, how it is with us, and how we should live. Can we, for example, climb to a high viewpoint from which we can see, clearly and as if from outside, what we are and how we are set in our world? Alternatively, can we perhaps find some fixed point of comparison vis-à-vis which to define ourselves?

Unfortunately, these attempts fail when we recognize that we live wholly inside our language, and our situation is therefore *outsideless*. We can't jump out of it, and we cannot compare it with anything else. We can only ever describe our condition *immanently*, from inside and without being able to find any antecedent presumption in favour of any one particular way of describing or constructing it.

Are we then stuck in a kind of linguistic relativism that never finds firm ground? No, because I am arguing that language, being what it is, is irrevocably committed to a certain vision of the world. It must attempt to build the world as a highly communicative society of mutually transparent persons, set in a humanly-appropriated world. Interestingly, the ideal world that language looks to is also the ideal world that is looked for at the end of time by both religion and political theory. And not only is language committed to a certain vision of the world (the communist society, heaven, Kant's 'kingdom of ends', the kingdom of God, etc.), but also we ourselves are irrevocably committed to language, as fish are to water. Therewith we are also committed to 'life' – that is, to time, to contingency, and to exchange with others.

Thus the three recent 'Everyday Speech' books have led me to the idea that the religion and philosophy of the future may be defended by a new sort of transcendental argument, as we see that the ordinary language in which we live binds us to a certain vision of the world and to a corresponding religious outlook.

Many thanks to the usual good friends, helpers, and fellow-travellers. On this occasion they have once again included Linda Allen and Hugh Rayment-Pickard.

Don Cupitt

Part One: Fore Words

Dogmatic theology and the philosophy of religion

During its long history theology has been many different things and has been taught in many different places – amongst them, the temple, the church, the monastery, the university and the denominational seminary. In one respect, however, theology has not changed, for it has always been an intensely practical subject: the account it gives of the gods and the supernatural world is supposed to bear very directly and with overriding authority upon the way we human beings are to understand ourselves, the way we live and the way we should direct our highest aspirations. Nobody would ever suppose that an account of the gods and their doings could be, or should even try to be, as objective and morally neutral as a work of natural history. On the contrary, theological statements have always been at least as much 'about' human beings and the human world as they have been 'about' spirit beings and the spirit world. Everything that is said in theology bears upon the vitally important moral relations between the two realms.

At first, a theology was an account of the gods. As such, it might include a *theogony*, an account of the genealogical relations amongst a system of gods, and a *theomachy*, an account of the power-struggles amongst the gods. Both of these themes survive prominently in Christian theology, which has a Father–Son relationship within God, and a rebellion in Heaven that is put down by loyalists. In addition, ancient theology assigned the various spheres of human life to the various gods, so that the pantheon, like human society, included rulers, lawgivers, warriors and farmers, and also gods who presided over fire and metalworking, and over the major cities and the various desirable qualities and virtues. The close correspondence between heavenly and earthly social organization meant that when a theologian or a poet synthesized a large body of mythology into a coherent story he was providing human social life with a parallel in the heavenly world – an ideal, founding and validating counterpart. Perhaps the most famous example of the way the parallelism was maintained is the fact that as the power of the city of Babylon increased in ancient Mesopotamia, so its god Marduk rose in the pantheon. Evidently the priests were well aware that the myths they recited in their temples were sending out a lot of very detailed messages about human social relations, messages that needed to be kept up to date.

In early Christianity the uses of the word 'theology' became still more specifically and closely related to human religious practice. Theology was the church's teaching about God; it was the naming of God, the formal recitation of, as one might say, the divine titles. It was the praise of God, and it was mystical knowledge of God.[1] Theology was thus a complex of discourses and practices through which the Christian could articulate his/her relationship to his/her own ultimate end, or life-goal. After about AD 500, under the influence of monasticism and the writings of people like the pseudo-Dionysius (*c.* 500), theology increasingly comes in effect to mean just mystical theology, or as we today might put it, spirituality. To understand the logic of God, to understand what is the status of language about God, one needed to engage with the religious life, and especially to practise contemplative prayer. The standard 'negative theology' warned that statements about God functioned, not to give us factual information about God, but to guide human spiritual life towards its goal.

The point here is so important that it deserves to be made again, with reference to the word 'ethics'. Originally *ethica* meant just customs, mores. But as the philosophical tradition developed, ethics came to deal with the whole question of how one should live, and in platonism ethics became something like a philosopher's version of religion, oriented towards the *Summum Bonum,* the highest good. In ethical discourse and practice one could articulate one's relationship to the good as the chief end or goal of life. Thus in the heyday of western culture one might say that ethics was the spirituality of the good: it showed the way to the good. And, correspondingly, theology was Christian spirituality, for it described the way to God – God being religion's way of representing the good as life's goal. All of this helps one to understand why 'Christian ethics' as a separate subject did not develop, and did not need to develop, for so long, why in the seventeenth century Spinoza's *Ethics* is a work of philosophical spirituality, and why Thomas Traherne's *Christian Ethics* of 1675 (the very first book with that title) is a work of spirituality and is subtitled 'the way to blessedness'.

Theology in its heyday, I am saying, was close both to philosophy and to ethics. All three subjects were teleological: in their somewhat different ways they all showed how a human being could find and follow the way to final, or 'eternal' happiness. This happiness was to be found in the vision of God (theology), in the highest good or *Summum Bonum* (ethics), and in the life of rational contemplation (philosophy). But in the twelfth century a certain religious loss occurred as Rome's power and claims increased, and theology became an academic subject studied in the new universities.[2] At Rome itself canon lawyers trained at the University of Bologna became dominant, and the Pope became a legal, rather than a religious figure – the absolute monarch of the church and the final court of appeal, the arbiter of what it was and was not lawful for a Christian to believe and to do. Theology became a branch of church law. Alternatively, at the University of Paris, where the great systematic theologies of the 'schoolmen' were written, theology became like a great gothic cathedral. It articulated the whole ideal culture of Christendom, a large and complex system of interconnected signs. Theology was the self-affirmation of a fully-developed religious civilization, continually seeking to define itself more clearly and to extend its own power. Henceforth the older, more mystical tradition would survive chiefly as a tradition of protest. It lived on as 'heresy'.[3]

Because the intellectual heritage of Christendom, as of Islam, included a substantial input from ancient philosophy, much was now made of the supposed fact that there was a body of religious truths that had reached us from two distinct sources independently. This body of truths was called 'natural theology', and was accessible to 'unassisted human reason', which meant that it could all be demonstrated simply by philosophical argument, while at the same time it had also been republished as part of divine revelation. The truths of natural theology were thus known twice over. They established the existence and nature of God, God's creation and providential government of the world, and also the existence of the rational human soul, with its inbuilt capability of knowing the natural moral law, its freedom, and its immortality. Natural theology was philosophy's bridgehead within theology, but you had to take care not to give the impression that you thought it could be religiously sufficient on its own. It couldn't be.

In breaking with Rome the Reformers largely rejected the authority both of tradition and of natural theology. Limiting the scope of theology to the biblical revelation, and putting printed copies of vernacular translations of the Bible into the hands of laypeople, the Reformers made their biblical theology into something very like what we would now call a political ideology. Its task was to train the individual to function as a citizen of the new Protestant nation-state. In the old Latin Church after the Council of Trent theology became something more like church ideology, something instilled into the clergy as part of their professional formation. By the nineteenth century theology was fast contracting and its general cultural importance was becoming minimal. Theology had become simply a subject in which Catholic seminarians, and Protestant trainees for the ministry and for teaching, had to pass examinations. As such it rapidly became largely descriptive and historical. It had little or nothing new to say any more, and on the creative side its functions were taken over by such new genres as the novel and utopian political theory.

As a living subject occupying a dominant position in both Protestant and Catholic cultures theology had run into crisis and broken down during the years 1780–1845. The great writers were all German: Kant, Fichte, Schopenhauer, Hegel, and the 'young Hegelian' critics of theology, D. F. Strauss, Ludwig Feuerbach and Karl Marx. The great events were chiefly British and French: the end of the old regime and the huge, surging power of the new commercial–industrial culture within the emergent liberal democratic state. In this new setting the old theological beliefs could no longer be held dogmatically and believed unquestioningly in quite the old way. Even their very intelligibility could no longer be taken for granted. They called first and foremost not for exposition, but rather for explanation.

So it came about that during the eighteenth century, as the old Christian culture and dogmatic theology declined, an almost entirely new subject, the philosophy of religion, gradually developed to replace it. The phrase first appears in book titles in Germany in the 1790s, and the best-known early texts are Kant's *Religion within the Limits of Reason Alone* (1793) and Hegel's courses of *Lectures on the Philosophy of Religion*, delivered in 1821, 1824, 1827 and 1831 at Berlin.[4] But the beginnings of the new subject can be traced back at least a century earlier, to Butler, to Locke and even to Pascal, for we are dealing here with a profound cultural shift. In the old hierarchical command-and-control type of culture all authority was absolute, all events were preordained, and religious truth was certain; but in the new commercial culture everything, from whether your ship will come home to how long you may expect to live, is seen only from the human point of view, and as subject to a human calculus of probabilities. In a market society, as Joseph Butler puts it, 'probability is the very guide of life';[5] your long-term well-being no longer depends upon the earnestness of your quest for absolute security, but upon your skill in calculating the odds and your readiness to venture your capital accordingly.

Himself a shopkeeper's son, Butler is well aware that in the coffee-houses of the city of London, where 'a great number of books and papers of amusement . . . of one kind and another, daily come in one's way', the old religious ways of thinking now play little part. Indeed, they are mocked:

It is come, I know not how, to be taken for granted, by many persons, that Christianity is not so much as a subject of inquiry; but that it is, now at length, discovered to be fictitious. And accordingly they treat it, as if, in the present age, this were an agreed point among all people of discernment; and nothing remained, but to set it up as a principal subject of mirth and ridicule, as it were by way of reprisals, for its having so long interrupted the pleasures of the world.[6]

This is an unpromising audience for an apologist to address, but Butler begins his big book by plunging straight into the subject of probability. The aim of his whole complex argument is to persuade his readers that we cannot be certain that Christianity is untrue, and that there is some finite probability that it is in fact true – indeed, quite enough to justify us in taking its claims very seriously.

It is difficult to emphasize sufficiently how different this is from the older way of thinking. In Christian culture faith had nothing to do with any calculation of odds. It was unconditional submission to absolute authority on the part of one who was assumed more than anything else to need the certainty of salvation. The meaningfulness and the truth of the propositions of divine revelation and dogmatic theology were certain. A relative liberal like Richard Hooker might qualify this a little by saying that the certainty of faith was moral certainty rather than metaphysical certainty, but he is miles away from Butler's Enlightenment readiness to concede the priority of the human world and the human viewpoint. One simply cannot imagine anyone before the Enlightenment looking coolly and as if from the outside at revealed religion as a scheme of thought, and forming a view as to its plausibility and the probability of its truth. The world was not like that, and people did not think in such terms, before the time of John Locke.

The late Ernest Gellner once made the point here by saying that before Kant human knowledge was set within the world, whereas after Kant the world was set within knowledge.[7] But we need to make the point in still more general terms, and push the changeover back to Locke, a century earlier: before the Enlightenment the scope of dogmatic theology was as wide as the whole culture. The individual was born naked into a pre-existent sacred cosmos, and confronted at once by all the ultimate things.[8] God and the whole epic of sin and salvation were all of them already out-there, overwhelming and tremendous facts. The word 'culture', as we use it today, did not exist. They didn't have culture, they had God. But with the Enlightenment everything comes to be seen from the human point of view. All cultural expression – religion, art, morality, science and so on – gradually comes to be seen as a human product and is appraised in terms of its effect upon the human subject.

Art is a good example. There was art, there was indeed great art, before the Enlightenment, but there was not art criticism or aesthetic theory as we now understand them. Only with Baumgarten is the need felt for both a theoretical account of the way works of art affect us, and a rationale for our judgments about the merits of works of art.[9] So with the Enlightenment we see the development of a whole set of philosophies-of. There are first the philosophies of perception and knowledge in general, and then the philosophies of all the major spheres of cultural life: the philosophies of law, politics, history, science, art, morality and religion. A large-scale and ambitious philosophical system will need to define and describe each of these spheres, and then to situate them in relation to each other on the whole map of culture. They may or may not be placed in order of rank, and they may or may not be totalized as in Hegel's version of absolute idealism, but it must already be clear that in the new era the status of theology has utterly and permanently changed. Dogmatic theology had formerly defined the 'absolute presuppositions' of a whole civilization. It really was the queen of the sciences. But now all the world is seen as held within human knowledge and is on the way to being regarded as a human construct. Religion has become just one human concern and one sphere of human cultural life amongst others. Religion is, in short, coming to be thought of as just human: humanly evolved, and carried within human language, within a human cultural tradition, and within certain institutions and sets of human cultural practices. Look out through your eyes at your present visual field. What has evolved historically is not chiefly all that stuff, out-there and seemingly independent of you, but rather the way your perception of it differentiates and interprets it all. Philosophy is about how we form our world of knowledge.

It is in this new context that the old grand style of dogmatic theology comes gradually to be replaced by a new subject: the philosophy of religion. It sees religion as an important but often very puzzling human cultural activity. It seeks to understand what religion is, and to place it in relation especially to politics, ethics and art. It asks what religious experience is, and what evidential or cognitive value it may have. By the 1840s, and especially amongst the German philosophers, it is becoming clear what the philosophy of religion is going to look like, and what range of options it will offer. Schleiermacher, Hegel, Feuerbach and Kierkegaard are the names to conjure with. And also by the 1840s, as the new situation dawns – well, begins to dawn – upon the old mainline churches, both Catholic and Protestant, it has become clear that the fundamental split within modern religious communities has already opened up. It is the split between the liberals, who broadly accept and want to work within the new conditions, and the traditionalists, who are desperate to find some way of reaffirming the old unconditional authority of revealed divine truth.

The obvious difficulty for the conservative dogmatic theologian who believes that there can be a revelation in language of divine truth to humans – who believes that he, though only human, can appropriate it without error and can work it up into a whole system of truth – is that he is claiming that a finite human mind can know 'the mind of God', can see and understand the truth from God's absolute and perspectiveless standpoint, and can speak with all the authority of God, whilst yet remaining himself, just a finite human being. In pre-critical times such a claim did not seem so absurd, because much the same claim was made by the old dogmatic rationalism in philosophy – by Leibniz and his followers, for example. But after Kant's critical philosophy it did seem absurd to claim that we can climb right out of ourselves and our own limitations and attain absolute religious knowledge, whilst yet remaining ourselves. In modern philosophy, 'the end of metaphysics' means amongst other things the abandonment of claims to absolute knowledge. We humans need henceforth to accept that all our knowledge is perspectival, mediated by language and fallible.

However, religious conservatives want to go on making a claim for dogmatic theology that philosophy has given up. It follows that they must see theology as radically outranking philosophy – which Karl Barth and his followers are happy to do. John Milbank, for example, declares that philosophy leads in the end to nihilism, whereas theology leads to absolute knowledge. And one must be prepared to accept all the implications of one's claim. Twenty years ago the Scottish dogmatic theologian T. F. Torrance read a paper in Cambridge setting out the whole gospel of the dogmatist. In the discussion that followed I asked him how he accounted for the widespread and intractable disagreements that plague theology. 'Sin,' he answered shortly (and doubtless with people like me in mind), and that was that.

The dogmatic theologian who maintains that there is in the end only one truth, that it has been revealed to humans, and that he is 'in' it, really must hold that the propositions of Islamic, or Latin Christian theology (as the case may be) are certain truths, and that as such they are qualitatively higher in epistemological rank than the propositions of (say) quantum theory. It is not surprising that such an outrageous claim becomes the subject of jokes. An old favourite tells of a Methodist minister and a Roman Catholic priest who are thrown together and become friends during the course of a cruise. They talk by the hour of many things. Then the cruise ends. In parting, the priest shakes hands with the minister, saying, 'So now we go back to our separate lives, you to worship God in your way, and I to worship him in his.'

Every joke has a date and a setting-in-life. That one, which clearly doesn't seem very funny any more, is in fact from the 1960s, a time when people could still acknowledge, half-mockingly and half-enviously, the old Roman dogmatic con- fidence. The joke is also obviously Anglican, both in being a little snooty about Methodists and in being uncomfortably aware of the seriousness of the modern polarization of religious thought between two mentalities, neither of which is entirely satisfactory. The only real position of their own that Anglicans have is the awareness of being permanently and embarrassingly suspended between two radically incompatible positions, strung up in limbo.

Here's another tale from the same period: from the published list of examiners, theology undergraduates at Cambridge deduced that in their finals their compulsory New Testament paper was going to be examined by a prominent liberal scholar. This figure was currently the Regius Professor of Divinity and Chairman of the Faculty Board, and they had a pretty good idea of his views. A delegation of Evangelical students called upon the Professor to lodge their protest. It was not right or fair that he should be their examiner, they complained, because he inter- preted the scriptures 'from Man's point of view, and not from God's'. Disarmingly, the professor confessed that he simply did not have access to any other point of view than the human one from which to judge such matters . . . and so on.

The story is a giveaway. It could have reached us only from the professor, because only he amongst those present could have per- ceived the situation as funny. To a serious-minded and recently converted young Evangelical Christian, whose mind is blessedly uncontaminated by mere human theories, it is quite beyond doubt that his/her own point of view and God's are one and the same. He/she has the mind of God, has been admitted in person to the knowledge of eternal verities and has nothing to learn from 'Man'. Roman Catholics may be almost habitually ironical, but Evangelicals are never so. They can't be. They know.

The difference between the two anecdotes is this: when we hear the first story we are conscious of feeling a little envy for the Roman priest, even though we know just on straightforward critical–historical grounds that his claims are untrue. One can see that acceptance of an absolute teaching authority might clear the decks and so make some (fairly attractive) versions of the religious life more pursuable. But when we hear the second story we don't feel any envy at all, only sadness that the once-great Protestant tradition has come down in the world so far, and so fast. Around the world, in Israel, in Egypt, in the USA and even in India, fundamentalist religion of one kind or another has become the ideology of the 'poor whites', the losers, the people who cannot cope with either modern thought or the new technologies. We may humour them, we may try to help them, but their ideas are not of a kind that we could ever take seriously – not in a million years. Yes, it is true that in the modern world, amongst certain Christians, Muslims, Jews and others, the old pre-Enlightenment sort of dogmatic confidence is still expressed here and there – but only by people who wilfully exclude all the counter-evidence from consideration.

Thus, it is possible for certain religious believers in various countries to be anti-darwinian 'creationists'; but the trick is done only by wilfully refusing to consider all the scientific evidence and arguments. Similarly, it is still possible for certain believers in various countries sincerely to hold that they have in their scriptures a written corpus of divinely-revealed truth, and that they themselves in person are so converted to that truth that they can rightly claim to have the mind of God and speak with the authority of God; but the trick is done only by their wilfully refusing to consider a whole series of points about language, interpretation and historical change that are (or should be) excruciatingly obvious to everyone who can use a good, big historical dictionary.

In this book I take the view that around the time of Hume and Kant in the eighteenth century dogmatism died, and the old style of Christian dogmatic theology perforce gave way to a new subject: the philosophy of religion. Where the older mentality still lingers, either it has to be consciously somewhat ironical about itself (as when the Pope jokes in private about his own infallibility, which he used to do), or it must fall into No-Nothing fundamentalism. What then about the Roman Catholic system? In a word, the position is this: as Slavoj Žižek has well put it, belief is always at first belief via a proxy, who believes on our behalf. The mind is not monological, as Descartes thought, but heterological: it works at one remove.[10] So the ordinary Catholic believes because the Pope believes, the Pope believes because the church believes – and the Pope on his own personal account? He is a little ironical. Work it out.

2

Globalization and religious thought

During the nineteenth century the philosophy of religion, as such and under that name, was not taught in British universities. But in Cambridge the subject was already acknowledged, at least to the extent that Butler and Paley were required reading, and when in 1904 teaching at last began for newly approved Theological Tripos papers in 'The Philosophy of Religion and Christian Ethics' it seemed appropriate that the syllabus should start from the old natural theology and the traditional concerns of apologetics.

A Stanton lectureship had been endowed to teach the new subject, and the first course of lectures shows what people at that time were worried about. Titled *Development and Divine Purpose*, it was delivered by V. F. Storr during the winter of 1904–05.[1] The chief problem it deals with is this: traditional Christian belief portrays world-events as ordained in every detail by Almighty God with a view to the fulfilment of his overall moral purpose. But throughout the nineteenth century people have more and more come to see the whole world-process, both in nature and in history, as unfolding in a purely immanent way without any external pre-planning or direction. The process of evolution by natural selection, for example, as it is described by evolutionary biologists, is neither pre-planned nor moral. There is no intelligent selector. Darwinism therefore seems to be quite incompatible with traditional belief in the providential government of world-events.

This is only one example of a whole series of challenges to the traditional religious cosmology that were being presented by the now-very-rapid growth of knowledge. Indeed, rapid and major historical change was threatening all traditional systems of thought, and perhaps especially Christian theology because of its longstanding alliance with platonism. Platonism is a notably anti-historical philosophy which subordinates everything in this shifting world below to an eternal world of general ideas, values and standards. For platonism, there can be no déep change, and the human situation is always and everywhere ultimately the same; whereas by the early twentieth century everyone was becoming aware of deep cultural differences and deep historical change. People were already asking how there could be a final revelation of divine truth within history. What is more, how can there be a progressive historical revelation of one timeless truth? Has not idealist philosophy already taken us far beyond the old belief in a personal God, and also beyond much else in Christian theology? Is not the whole Christian era already receding into the past?

Thus from its first beginnings as a formal academic subject in the year 1904 the philosophy of religion was seen as concerned almost solely with Christianity, and in particular with Christian apologetics. Its syllabus consisted of the old natural theology syllabus, modified and supplemented to reflect current anxieties. Accordingly, it found itself dealing with the relation of faith to history, religious language, religious experience and questions to do with the relation of God to the world: providence, miracles, prayer and the problem of evil. Such was the syllabus I studied in the mid-1950s, and taught until the mid-1990s: it called itself 'the philosophy of religion', but it might have been more aptly labelled 'current issues in Christian apologetics'.[2] It studied stock arguments, traded back and forth, about stock issues – many of which had long since ceased to interest real philosophers.

The problem of evil was a clear example. It arises as a problem only for people who have been taught to believe that world-events are controlled by a benevolent Providence that has foreseen and foreordained everything, so that nothing irretrievably disastrous should happen to good and innocent folk like ourselves. That is, the problem of evil is not a problem in philosophy, but merely a problem within theology. Philosophers in the main do not encounter it, because they do not start from the assumption that we are entitled to expect world-events to run in such a way as to protect the good and innocent, and punish the wicked. They are more likely simply to note that there is a very large element of contingency in the way things go, and that all of us are liable suddenly to be struck by tragedy or misfortune. The fact that the problem of evil has bulked so large in the philosophy of religion shows that the subject has hitherto been a branch of theology rather than of philosophy, and that it has been studied against the background of a rather naively realistic and populist understanding of orthodox Christian doctrine.

Things began visibly to change in the 1970s, and although the changes are biting slowly, they are biting very deep.

English as the first globalized language and culture

Until as recently as the 1950s there was an English culture, and many or most of the premier English-language writers were still rooted in it. But since the later 1950s the English language has been twice decentred, first by the removal of its controlling centre to the United States, and then secondly by a further removal of its centre away from concrete social life and into 'the web' of new technologies. Microsoft has recently sponsored the publication of the first dictionary of this new world-English, the principal language of cyberspace.[3]

Within England itself this decentring of our language has severely affected all the institutions and persons that used to be concerned with forging and celebrating the connections between England's language, culture and national identity. Many of the younger members of the royal family no longer speak the Queen's English, the Church of England can no longer market itself to the nation as being, through its Bible and its liturgy, the chief repository of the national spirit, and there is no living writer whose work symbolizes and celebrates Englishness in quite the old way. Much of English writing is no longer grounded in English social life. Our best writers are post-nationalist, not least because, like Indian writers in English, they know that they must

sell chiefly overseas. England and her language have become profoundly post-modernized – decentred, multi-ethnic, scattered.
We are citizens of the world, who prefer the Dalai Lama to
choral Evensong, and we are not complaining. We are – most of
us – rather happy to have been delivered from our previous
confinement within a local tradition that was only occasionally
first-rate, and more often was stultifyingly mediocre.

Within the academic world corresponding changes have
already taken place. Thus at Cambridge the university itself was
a national institution, which equipped young men to go out and
'serve God in Church and State'. The Divinity Faculty was
almost wholly staffed by Anglican priests who also served as
college Deans, and it saw itself as a Faculty of Christian Theology. Today the university is rather consciously international,
welcoming members of both sexes and every nation, and the
Divinity Faculty teaches 'theology and religious studies', with
lecturers in Judaism, Islam, Hinduism and Buddhism. There are
still many people who cling to the old ecclesiastical domination
of the agenda for the subject called 'theology', and truly post-
ecclesiastical theologians are still in the minority; but it is
obvious that major change has already occurred and will continue. It will eventually require the wholesale revision of sylla-
buses.

We have long thought of ourselves as obsessive traditionalists,
who dislike large-scale blueprints for reform and prefer everything to be untidy and historically evolved – as indeed are our
language, our common law and our constitution. It was David
Hume who first called us 'the historical nation', for that reason.
But the generation of young British artists who emerged around
1990 in London showed by their almost total rejection of history
how post-modernized we have now become. Damien Hirst and a
few others produced highly innovative works that were unlike
almost any previous art, but which nevertheless did quickly
establish themselves as art. It was arguably the first time the
British had ever led the world in art, even if only briefly. And this
leads one to hope that our post-modernization, and the rapid
decay of all the traditional vehicles and foci of our national

identity, may make possible similarly revolutionary changes in religious thought.

Religious thought urgently needs to overcome – even to 'destroy', in Heidegger's sense – its own history and its own received vocabulary. English is, happily for our present purpose, the right language for the job.

The end of the world religions

It is often supposed that the philosophy of religion can easily globalize itself by simply drawing back a few paces, and giving itself a wider field of view. Instead of attending solely to the Judaeo–Christian tradition, it should address itself to religion and the history of religions in general, and to the philosophical traditions of Islam, India and East Asia as well as of Europe. Hegel was perhaps the first major writer to see the need for, and to attempt, a globalized, multi-faith philosophy of religion.[4] But like Troeltsch and Tillich in more recent times, he still wanted to reserve a special status for Christianity as being in some sense the 'absolute' religion.[5] Others have tried to be more impartial, unifying their philosophy of religion around some supposed common core.

There are four main theories about what this common core of all religion is. For Aldous Huxley and many others it is 'the perennial philosophy', which turns out to resemble neo-platonism. For Rudolf Otto it is the sense of 'the Numinous', or the Holy.[6] For W. T. Stace, Huston Smith and others, it is the unitive mystical experience.[7] Finally, for John Hick and other multi-faith monotheists, all true religion shares a common orientation towards 'the real', which may be experienced either as God or (in East Asia) as the Absolute.[8]

The very fact that at least four different accounts of the essence of religion are forthcoming should set alarm bells ringing and, in fact, we can be pretty confident that we will from now on hear no more about a supposed common core of religion. The very quest for a common core is 'essentialist', and essentialism is surely as obviously a mistake in the case of religion as it is in the case of art. In modern times art in the West has been characteristically anti-essentialist; that is to say, each notable new movement in art has derived its imaginative shock and its artistic impetus precisely from the way it has rebelled against and overthrown the then-received understanding of what art is. The nature of art is, it now seems, continually to escape from itself and redefine itself. And in exactly the same way, the history of religions is full of innovators, reformers, iconoclasts and prophets who make religion exciting and interesting again precisely by the way in which they rebel against and successfully overthrow current ideas of what true religion is. Every good new thing in religion began life as a sharp reaction against the status quo. Just as the liveliest and most exciting art is anti-essentialist about art, so too the liveliest and most challenging religious teachers are always anti-essentialist about religion. As the great Ch'an teachers might have put it,[9] there is indeed a 'great matter' that religion is all about, but every attempt to bring it forward into clear focus, to specify it, or to pin it down needs instantly to be challenged. The great matter needs to be attended to, not yakked about. True religion needs continually to war against essentialism and idolatry. And one might add that the great historical diversity of religion, and the incommensurability of the several vocabularies of the major traditions, teaches the same lesson.

So this is the law: if any particular specification of the common core of all true religion ever comes to prevail in public debate, it will immediately become the religious duty of the serious religious writer to declare war upon it and try to overthrow it. 'What today is religion, tomorrow will be atheism: and what today is atheism, tomorrow will be religion.'

We are considering the typically late-modern claim that in an age of cultural globalization the philosophy of religion can solve its problems by going multi-faith and identifying the common core of all true religion everywhere. Following in the tradition of Plato's essentialism, there have been several proposed definitions of the common core; but they have all failed, and we are not likely to hear much more of them, for they don't fit the facts and in any case there is an important religious objection to all of them. The religious object, the 'great matter' with which religion is concerned, is in some way outside language and cannot be satisfactorily specified in language. It is systematically elusive, and must remain so. One should not talk about it: one should let it be.

The argument so far has two corollaries. The first is very simple: although on the current reckoning there are between eight and twelve 'world religions', only between three and five of them even purport to be universal or 'catholic' in their missionary outreach to the whole human race, namely Christianity, Islam and Buddhism. (To these three we may wish to add that there have been in modern times attempts to establish the Bahai faith and Hinduism as universal faiths; and in addition a few other faiths, notably Judaism and Zoroastrianism, have been proselytizing at some times in their past history.) So there are indeed a few purportedly universal faiths, but they all face the problem that they are limited by being locked to their own very local origins and early development. If we were to try to break Christianity out of its Jewish background and Graeco–Roman formative period, if we were to try to imagine a post-Arabic Islam and if Buddhism were to become totally westernized and to break its links back to its various local Asian traditions, then in each case people would complain that the faith had 'lost its identity'. Catholic and would-be universal religious traditions turn out to have ties back to a particular place of origin, a particular sacred language and a particular cultural tradition that they cannot shed.[10] All attempts to demythologize away 'the scandal of particularity' turn out in the end to be self-defeating. In this case none of the 'world religions' can really be 'world' to the extent that our science, technology, democratic politics and humanitarian ethics are now 'world'. Globalization seems to transcend or go beyond all the world religions alike, and invites us to wonder what form a post-ethnic and truly global religion might one day take.

The classic example of this is the great earthquake which struck north west Turkey on 17 August 1999. Somewhat to their own surprise, the Greeks found themselves sending humani-

tarian aid at once, in a manner and a spirit which suddenly over-
came five hundred years of very bitter antagonism between
Christians and Muslims, and within a week had changed relations between the two countries. Nothing could have shown the
world more clearly how powerful a moral and political force
the new global humanitarianism can be and, by contrast, how
quickly and completely great old religious issues and conflicts
can be superseded and eclipsed by it.

This brings us to the second corollary of our argument against
essentialism: the very notion of a plurality of world religions,
which are to be laid out for inspection, to be described and compared as social and historical phenomena, and to be viewed from
an ideal and universal philosophical standpoint independent of
them all – all this has already profoundly decentred and dis-
placed religion. Too much objective historical study, too much
scientific theorizing about it, causes people to miss the point of
religion, in a way that is dangerous. A Ch'an story makes the
point with typical simplicity.

> When a monk asked the master (i.e. Huang Po) 'What is the
> meaning of coming from the West?', the master hit him with
> his staff.[11]

Maybe this story calls for a little explanation: Huang Po is a
Chinese Buddhist master of the ninth century. Buddhism had
entered China 'from the West', from India some eight centuries
earlier, the legendary apostle of China being the monk
Bodhidarma. The disciple is thus raising an historical question
about Chinese Buddhist origins – and Huang Po hits him, by way
of saying, 'That's not the point, that's not what we are here for,
that is a dangerous distraction.' And to return to our present
discussion, *Religionsgeschichte*, the history of religions and the
comparative study of religion, like the critical–historical study of
scripture in Christian theology, systematically trains the student
to objectify religion and to miss the point of it. In our faculties of
theology students are trained to get it all wrong, which is why
Kierkegaard was right to fear that critical–historical study of

scripture and Christian origins would bring about the decline of religion.[12] It has. And nowadays the subject called Religious Studies, or the Comparative Study of Religions, is making the same mistake at the global level. Globalization, like computerization, is usually associated with the triumph of commodified knowledge and the universalizing, theoretical and scientific gaze, whereas religion, like humour, is different. It is usually highly context-dependent, particular and *ad hominem*. Suddenly, one sees everything from a new angle, suddenly one is cut to the quick, suddenly one gets the point, suddenly it all makes sense and it's all worthwhile.

From this discussion I conclude that the notion of a set of 'world religions', each with its own sacred territory (Christendom, Islam, Hindustan, etc.) and carving up the whole inhabited world between them, is a mistake. It arose in the Enlightenment, and in its outworkings reflects the process of what Derrida has called 'globalatinization',[13] which in the present context means the desire to construct every other religion on the model of the Latin, or Roman Catholic, church. Every other religion has also to be a 'creed', every other religion has also to have a supranational level of organization and a orderly pyramid of spiritual power; every other religion has to be divided between an officer class and the footsoldiers, the clergy who control truth and worship, and the laity; every other religion has to have its own group of heartlands, its own territory and so on. To this day westerners insist, for example, upon viewing the Dalai Lama as a sort of combination of Christ and the Pope. However often he may declare that he is only a simple Buddhist monk, we want to view him as an incarnate god, a 'god-king' and a spiritual ruler. It is routinely assumed by western journalists that he must, of course, also be a theist. And it is taken for granted that prior to the arrival of western influences Tibet, like Ethiopia or like mediaeval Europe, was a picturesque, peaceful and homogeneous sacred civilization. Globalatinization makes us think this way, but it was never true. Buddhism in particular never had and still does not have any supranational level of organization at all. It isn't even quite nationally organized. It exists and always has existed only as a plurality of 'sects': local folk customs, the spheres of influence of local monasteries and teaching lineages and so on. Although, of course, excessive deference to authority is as likely to be found in Buddhism as in any other tradition, Buddhism does not have any priesthood as such, and never quite becomes 'organized religion' in the western sense. There is no Buddhist church, and no hierarchy that claims supranational jurisdiction, and the Dalai Lama's Lhasa version of Buddhism was never the only one even in Tibet. On the contrary, there were in Tibet many relics of pre-Buddhist religion, there were many different schools of Buddhist thought and teaching associated with different monasteries and there was, of course, a huge gap between popular religious practice and the highly refined philosophical Buddhism of a few leading monks.[14] So in an important sense Buddhism, the big essence and the organized ideological bloc, does not exist and never did exist.

One may add to this that there is a similar gap between our idealized perception of Prester John's Abyssinian Christian Empire, an harmonious sacred civilization, and the very untidy actuality of the history of Christianity in Ethiopia, in which there were always conflicts between many different strands of thought, and in which many large ethnic groups in the population were never Christian at all. Even odder, and by way of turning globalatinization against itself, there is a sound and clear sense in which the Roman Catholic Church is itself a recent invention, for it is only since the nineteenth century that the usages of the diocese of Rome and the monarchical rule of the Bishop of Rome have at last been imposed in a really thoroughgoing way upon the whole Latin church, over-riding all the old local authorities, laws, customs and liturgies. The highest achievement of *pax romana* is the universal consent of the faithful to Rome's absolute authority: everything is transparently classified, regulated and ranked in terms of its spiritual power. Fine, maybe, but its achievement in the West is very recent. (What everyone thinks of as 'Roman Catholicism' is surprisingly recent: try to date the phrase, just that phrase.) The past was different, and other traditions were and are different. Before modern communications and before printing one could scarcely dream of creating that sort of uniformity and that sort of universal control of truth and conduct.

The end of the western canon

In the past, religious and philosophical writing almost always moved within boundaries, used technical terms and referred to landmarks that were tacitly agreed between writer and reader. The two – writer and reader – belonged to the same tradition, and it was usually easy for the reader to pick up the cues. Great names were mentioned, the argument threaded its way between various well-known hazards and blind alleys, some things did not need saying and other things were left conspicuously unsaid and so on. There was a good deal of complicity between writer and reader and upon this complicity the very intelligibility and interest to the reader of the text largely depended.

The question arises of how this very useful complicity was created – and the answer is surely that in the cultural milieu common to both reader and writer there were recognized canons of standard works with which one could presume familiarity. These classical writers between them had marked out the playing field and established the rules of the game. They had bequeathed to their successors a repertoire of standard moves and counter-moves, 'positions', landmarks and traps. To study them was to become skilled in the subject, and to study their historical succession was perhaps a way of working out in what direction the subject should be taken next.

Here we notice that the background canon·not only makes intelligible the work of orthodox academicians who are happy to work within the received tradition, but is equally necessary to make intelligible the work of revolutionary innovators. Revolutionaries cannot possibly be understood unless we know what they are rebelling against and why. Both the 'conservative' and the 'radical' need the canon in the background to make their work intelligible. And this would seem to be true not only in philosophy, theology, the visual arts and music, but perhaps also in science. In the case of science the difference is that once the revolutionary theorist has brought about his paradigm shift, the older tradition can be set aside and forgotten, except by historians. To understand Galileo's achievement, one needs to understand the Aristotelian physics that he was arguing against and its still-formidable social power in his day. But a century later, in the heyday of Newton, it was no longer necessary to trouble oneself very much with the older world-view. Knowledge of a long-established canon of great practitioners is valuable indeed, but it isn't so essential to the training of scientists and the understanding of science as it is to the formation of composers, philosophers and theologians. Once again we are prompted to think that philosophy and theology are closer in spirit and in method to the fine arts than they are to natural science.

Philosophy and theology then are both subjects that have, and seem to need, a canon. One does not usually begin the study of natural science by studying the history of science, but one does usually begin the study of theology and philosophy by studying at first hand a number of canonical texts, many of them dating from the first origins of the subject in classical antiquity. What is more, we in the West have since early modern times been highly ethnocentric about our traditions. We have simply equated the history of philosophy with the history of western philosophy, and the western canon has been for us the canon absolutely. Similarly, 'theology' has been western or Latin Christian theology, theology as written by Paul, Augustine, Thomas Aquinas, Luther, Calvin and Barth, and the Art Gallery has contained specimens of west European art only. Non-western works of art were until well after 1900 regarded as curios and kept in a different museum.

Western ethnocentrism was not always so extreme as it eventually became. In the early Middle Ages Byzantine art was very readily received and admired in the West, and Thomas Aquinas treats with great respect the views of leading Jewish and Arab philosophers such as Maimonides and Avicenna (Ibn Sina). Italian paintings attest a knowledge of and liking for Persian rugs and Chinese ceramics that goes back to 1600 and earlier. But as western Europe became politically dominant over most of the globe, so an assumption of west European cultural hegemony developed. On the basis of remarkable achievements, especially in philosophy and music, there could even be in the late nineteenth century an assumption of German cultural hegemony over all the rest of humankind.

We need not here become embroiled in the story of the catastrophic events that ended Europe's supremacy. Suffice it to say that from now on we should not make the mistake of assuming that the western canon is *the* Canon, absolutely, either in philosophy or in theology. We cannot so confidently as before conscript the rest of humankind into our own cultural tradition, or expect them to be grateful for walk-on parts in our expansionist myth about ourselves. The whole notion of a canon – who draws it up, and in what interest? – has become questionable. Inevitably, there are serious knock-on effects for both philosophy and theology as subjects.

The end of the old confidence about the western canon calls into question the old cosy complicity – the set of tacit assumptions, shared by writer and reader, upon which the very intelligibility of philosophical and theological writing largely rested. In some respects, those assumptions were unhealthy. They too easily assumed that the rest of the world could be disregarded. Is it not odd that so many of our twentieth-century western philosophers and theologians have been – and still are – more parochial in our time than St Thomas Aquinas was in the thirteenth century? Indeed, between the eighth and the thirteenth centuries there was much more intellectual contact between Christians and Muslims than there has been in recent times, despite the wars between them in those days.

But there is a further and more serious reason why the end of the old confidence about the western canon creates a new and very uncertain situation. Western philosophy was described summarily by Whitehead as 'footnotes to Plato', and Christian theology has been if anything even more heavily indebted to platonism than has the philosophical tradition. The end of the canon exposes a series of deep, broadly platonic assumptions, and forces us to ask ourselves how we can learn to function without them. I mention three of them here.

First, there is the assumption of the primacy of knowledge. What does a human being need most of all? Some might answer with the Buddha: deliverance from unhappiness and confusion. Others might say with Freud, 'love and work': personal fulfilment by making a worthwhile contribution to society for which one is given due social recognition. Platonism answers simply, knowledge: lucid, contemplative and blessed knowledge of a supremely real and valuable object.

This assumption of the primacy of knowledge remains very strongly held amongst Christians and post-christians of every sort in the West, from the most conservative Roman Catholics to the most populist Evangelicals: before all else, the Christian must hold the correct doctrinal beliefs. They are the *sine qua non*.

Second, there is the assumption of a need to be delivered from everything that is 'merely' temporal, finite and contingent. This account of what it is that we need to be redeemed from is evidently linked to the contrast between the apparent and the real. The visible world in which our lives are set, the world in which everything is 'merely' temporal, finite and contingent, is described as the world of appearance, or of becoming. It is contrasted with the higher world of eternal, infinite and necessary reality or being. To be happy, we need to live all our life as a journey through time towards our final home in the eternal world.

And third, along with the contrast between the eternal world above and the merely temporal and visible world below, there is the old contrast between two different spheres or realms, the sacred and the profane. The sacred realm has existed as a distinct and specially authoritative sphere of social life for about five or six thousand years, so that it is older than platonism. We should see Plato as having translated the ancient sacred/profane distinction into philosophical language, which was duly borrowed back again for their own use by Christian, Jewish and Muslim theologians.

These assumptions between them generated our long-established two-worlds dualism. The unseen sacred world was constructed as a 'spiritual' counterpart or parallel to the visible profane and human world. This was done by taking the ordinary human vocabulary for describing this-worldly goings-on and bending it a little, so as to preserve both the close analogy between the two realms and the infinite qualitative difference between them.

Thus the process of this-worldly human existence was called life, and its enhanced parallel in the sacred world was called eternal life. Profane love might be called *eros*, erotic or sexual love, and its sacred counterpart would then be described as *agape* or 'charity'. We see things in the visible world with a mortal eye, the eye of flesh, and we see things in the sacred world with an inward eye, the eye of spiritual understanding. And so on: writing constantly hammered home both the intimate analogy and the qualitative difference between things human and things divine, between the carnal and the spiritual. There are for example both earthly and spiritual fathers, but whereas every earthly father needs a spouse, in Catholic Christianity it was understood that no spiritual father, neither priest, nor bishop nor God himself, can possibly have a spouse.

The two-worlds cosmology having been set up, the next step is to acknowledge that the split between the two worlds is painful and cannot be ultimate. Our redemption requires the healing of the rift. Christ in his own person bridges the gap between the worlds, and is the promise of their ultimate unification. But it is not bridged yet: in this life it continues, and religious writing continues to insist upon it.

Now what happens to religious writing when the old western canon breaks down? The belief in the possibility of absolute visionary knowledge, the old two-worlds dualism, and the old distinction between the sacred and the profane realms, all lose their traditional philosophical unpinning, which had seemed fairly secure from Plato to Kant – that is, from about 400 BC to AD 1800. So what does happen next? Do religious beliefs become simply unintelligible?

The obvious answer, in much religious thought since Blake

and Hegel, is that Christianity completes its own historical development, and the two worlds become fully interfused again. The death of God coincides with the salvation of the lower world, for when the sacred world comes back down into the profane world, our delighted eyes learn to see this life as our eternal life, eros as agapeic, every family as the Holy Family, the fresh wind as divine breath or spirit, every night as a vigil, every dawn as Advent, and the whole visual field as a divine revelation, saturated with religious significance. A recent newspaper reports the case of a woman whose sight has just been restored by surgery, after twenty years of blindness. Amazed at the glory of the visual field, she said simply 'My God!' Precisely. Cutting out the two-and-a-half millennia of metaphysics and two-worlds dualism, religious writing will poetize ordinariness again, as perhaps it did in archaic times.

That being so, the philosophy of religion will lay out the possibility-conditions for religious writing. It will describe how post-modern philosophy sees language, the self, other selves and the world and this account will lead on to the constructive theology that shows in detail how religious writing can transform and redeem the world and human lives.

The result will be a religious outlook rather different from the old one. When religious symbols are filled out and explained in terms of platonic philosophy the result is a religious outlook that combines two-worlds dualism with a two-stage redemption. We live after Christ's death and resurrection, which promise the eventual enosis of the two worlds into one again, but we live in the period of waiting for the final fulfilment of that promise. The period of waiting is the epoch of ecclesiastical Christianity, which will end – but not just yet. Such was the old outlook, but today we are changing over to a new one-world religious outlook in which religious writing does not describe supernatural facts at all, but instead simply seeks to poetize and redeem this world now. The philosophy of religion then aims to show how this can work, after having first given its own account of the relevant bits of general philosophy. Its religion may still owe much to historic ecclesiastical Christianity, but it will no longer need or have any distinctively or exclusively Christian labels. The idea of 'religions' as mutually exclusive spiritual nationalities, so that when you confess allegiance to one you exclude all the others, is dead. In the globalized world religious (and ethnic) differences get less and less important. Global religion is at last truly catholic or universal.

Such is, roughly, my prospectus in this book. But there is an obvious snag, which I can illustrate with an anecdote. Around 1960, at a certain theological college, there was an enthusiastic young ordinand who had already seized upon the early-1960s idea that Christian action both secularizes the sacred, making holy things common, and sacralizes the secular, making profane things holy. When he looked about him in the college dining hall, he thought that every common meal that we ate together should be treated as a eucharist. And when he looked about him in the college chapel, it occurred to him that the religious significance of the eucharist would become much clearer if instead of being a merely ritual meal with a wafer and a sip, it were celebrated as a real fellowship meal, with a big hunk of bread and a full draught of wine. In short, the platonic separation between symbolic holy meals in the chapel and real profane meals in the dining hall was wrong. So he campaigned one week for the effective conversion of the dining hall into the chapel and then the next week for the effective conversion of the chapel into the dining-hall.

Now even in a theological college, even at that time, people were capable of putting two and two together. They began to make ribald comments. Did not his two moves, the one trying to make every meal into a eucharist and the one trying to make every eucharist into a real meal, cancel each other out? Would we not in any case all become rather bloated? Besides, when his programme was complete, there would be no detectable difference between what was happening in the chapel and what was happening in the dining hall. Why keep two separate rooms, for what had become only one purpose? One unreconstructed Anglo–Catholic amongst us suggested that the late-modern programme of secularizing Christianity would end by leaving us with nothing to say except that ordinariness is fine as it is. We'd be like those Wittgensteinians who renounce metaphysics and simply say 'yes' to ordinary life. Is that, in the end, all that Christianity has to say?

Let's take this further. During the 1960s and since then, a large number of Roman Catholic priests became laicized, married and started families. At first they were utterly thrilled to discover how straightforwardly wholesome and holy is the whole business of marriage, sex and babies. As objects of devotion, a real woman and children are a huge improvement on Mary and the Holy Family. But the initial effect of magic cannot last forever and as the decades pass ordinariness becomes, well, just ordinary.

Now the dilemma can be stated. It would seem that religious language needs the illusions of platonism in order to sustain its intelligibility and its symbolic effectiveness. For if everything is brought down into this world and ordinariness, then the magical life-enhancing effect of religious metaphors must gradually fade and there will be only banality. As my unreconstructed Anglo–Catholic friend used to put it, 'You can't plonk on every syllable.' The choice in the end is between the noble lie of platonism and other-worldly religion and mere banal ordinariness. And what is more, exactly the same dilemma can be demonstrated within middle-way Buddhism. Ever since Nagarjuna there has been a line of argument that wants to equate *nirvana* with *samsara*, the religious goal with ordinariness. And here again we are left wondering if in the end religion can have nothing to recommend to us except a quietistic acceptance of the world of everyday life.

Is that true?

3

On systematic 'closure'

From the earliest times – and that means, at least since the Upper Palaeolithic, and perhaps much earlier than that – human beings have sought to improve their understanding and control of events by detecting and defining regular patterns in the world of experience. Notches on bones attest early attempts to define the calendar and bone flutes show early human interest in fixing musical scales. Analogies and sympathies between the cosmic order and human life were noted very early: they include the fitting of the human rhythm of waking and sleeping to the cosmic cycle of day and night, the analogy between the twenty-eight-day reproductive cycles of women and of the moon, and the way hunter–gatherers must learn to follow the annual rhythms of plants and animals, which in turn follow the seasons and the sun.

Against this background, it is not surprising that so much of the history of thought has been devoted to attempts to find or to impose a unified rational order, not just within the flux of natural phenomena, but also within the self. People have struggled to impose order upon their own lives, and to achieve in themselves a unified consciousness under the sovereignty of reason, in the very deeply held belief that the 'noumenal' or intelligible reality underlying everything was one, regular and perfect. By clarifying and ordering the self, one might hope to become more closely attuned to the unseen controlling powers.

A whole series of analogies were commonly invoked here. As the logos, the principle of intelligibility, is to the cosmos, so the monarch is to the state, the human soul to the body, and its meaning to the text. The general idea is that a complex domain is unified under the government of a transcendent rational prince or principle that regulates it, and whose authority bears on every part of it. And a corollary of this general idea is the very intriguing and seductive thought that reality itself is an intelligible system that might be adequately copied and represented in a book – the Book of Everything. A systematic literary work is able to copy a law-governed natural system because (it is often believed) the world itself has been formed by language, so that there is a natural isomorphism between sentences and states of affairs. This isomorphism makes it possible for language to copy reality precisely.

It is also to be noticed here that there is a close relationship between system and power, summed up neatly in the phrase 'everything under control'. The more completely and transparently the ruling prince or principle orders everything within the domain, the greater his or its manifest power.

Now, many of these considerations still figure prominently in religious thought. Systems of religious belief and bodies of holy tradition always present themselves as one, rational and complete. Codified – that is, assembled and organized into a codex, a book – the body of sacred doctrine or of the Law is a *plenum*. Nothing can be added to it, and nothing may be subtracted from it: it is 'sufficient for our salvation', and a complete and perfect guide to human life. Against that background it has been common for people to regard their sacred scriptures as containing divinely revealed truths. Given that we have a set of such divine truths, it is not at all surprising that theologians using standard logic should set about working them up into a system of absolute or objective knowledge. The theological system gives us humans access to the very mind of God, the order he has imposed upon the world, and his will for our salvation. Theology was once as grand a subject as that.

In one way or another, then, the idea of an objective systematic unity of truth, whether in the mind of God or in the objective rational unity of the cosmic order, has since early times inspired human beings to seek themselves to gain a similarly systematic personal knowledge of the truth, in natural philosophy or physics, in metaphysics, in systematic theology or by systematizing God's revealed law. The idea of a complete and perfect, 'closed' or rounded-off system of knowledge is endlessly seductive. People feel that to achieve it would be to gain happiness, and even today there are, as everyone knows, still people who say that to achieve a complete fundamental science of nature would be 'to know the mind of God'.

Observe that the notion of systematic 'closure' is highly theological. In God there are no loose ends. God is simple and timeless, and knows everything in one, at once, without being in any way dependent upon anything else to complete his knowledge. The believer who draws near to God hopes that in knowing God he will come to see 'all things in God'; that is, participate in God's omniscience.

So runs the dream, both of traditional theistic faith and of rationalist philosophy. But there are some fatal objections to it. One of them was observed early in the history of German idealism: God has always been believed to be, not just a rational system, but spirit, i.e. masterfully conscious. God is not just an *a priori* truth, something self-intelligible. He doesn't just know everything: he is spirit, that is, he knows that he knows everything. In which case he cannot just be simple, or – as it was put – 'pure act', wholly centred within himself and exactly coinciding with himself. Consciousness implies a certain lack, a certain inner distancing of the self from itself, within the self, and therefore an element of complexity that is incompatible with God's simplicity. So there is a fatal internal contradiction within the traditional philosophy of God, which perhaps only Spinoza was smart enough to see and avoid (and he was very far from being an orthodox theist).[1]

There is a second fatal flaw in the idea of God. It has to do with the claim that God is an absolute and eternal mind, in whom all knowledge is 'totalized' and unified, autonomously, without any remainder and without any outside. This evidently implies that every bit of God's knowledge is completely consistent and transparent to God and in God, without being dependent upon anything that is external to or independent of God. But in 1931

Kurt Gödel published a paper in symbolic logic in which he demonstrated that any and every formal system or pure calculus rich enough to include arithmetic must contain propositions that are not provable within the system.[2] This immediately makes it doubtful whether it makes sense to claim that God is an absolute, autonomous mind that perfectly comprehends all things – including himself – in one timeless and purely rational vision, without any loose ends, or remainders, or outside. In more recent philosophy there has been much amplification of this point, echoing the doubts that Kierkegaard expressed about Hegel's System. Do not time and contingency immediately threaten every system, beginning to erode it from the instant that it is completed? Is there not always bound to be something left unthought, something left unproved, some remainder that the System has not managed to incorporate? Is not the knowledge of finite biological organisms like ourselves always perspectival, and always structured or ordered by our own merely contingent priorities; and is it not somehow intrinsic to the very nature of language that the final truth and the very last word are never quite reached?

There is further difficulty: in the classical account as given by, for example, Leibniz, the world is fully determinate, and what appear to us as contingent, 'synthetic' truths about the world are all of them necessary and 'analytic' truths in God. Furthermore, they are of course all mutually consistent. Thus Leibniz seeks to reconcile the complexity of the world with the divine necessity and simplicity; and his account seemed to work in relation to early modern physics. But in our present physics the world is shot through with random elements and indeterminacy in a way that surely cannot be overcome in God along Leibnizian lines. Coarsely put, God cannot both play dice and not play dice. One and the same situation cannot be both in principle indeterminate from our point or view, and yet fully determinate and necessary in the divine mind.

These considerations suggest that there is something badly wrong with the idea of total, completely unified and autonomous knowledge of a fully determinate world. We'd do better to say no more than that everything is contingent and interconnected, and acknowledge that the world can be described in any number of ways, just as there is no specifiable upper limit to the number of possible English sentences.

A dilemma thus arises, for both philosophy and theology are intensely attracted by the idea of systematically complete knowledge.[3] Philosophy usually distinguishes itself by its attempt to achieve complete generality, thinking its way all round a topic and considering it from every angle. Theology has always been lured and tempted by the view that equates final salvation with the complete intellectual satisfaction and happiness that we will find in the vision of God. All our doubts and questionings will be put to rest for ever when we see all things in God, and see that everything is now and eternally exactly as it must be and should be. Here in this life, when we strive for systematic coherence in a philosophical or religious text, we are looking for something that will give us a foretaste of that eternal happiness.

Unfortunately it now seems that we look in vain. In philosophy, Hegel's production of his grand visionary system coincided with the first suggestions, by Schelling and Schopenhauer, that noumenal reality might not after all be one and perfect, but might on the contrary be somewhat alienated from itself, and even eternally divided against itself. By the end of the nineteenth century people are beginning to give up the idea that there is somehow a pre-established harmony between 'thought and being', or between language and reality, and also to give up the idea that we are entitled to expect all truth to be totalizable into a grand systematic unity. Why do we expect such things? Why, for example, did Kant feel so strongly obliged and entitled to hope for the ultimate harmonization of morality and nature, although the conflict between them as he describes it is obviously irreconcilable? Today the old systematic dream is dead in philosophy, and looks very wobbly in theology. It is dead, surely, even amongst fideists such as the followers of Karl Barth, who are the last remaining people who still think of attempting a systematic theology. Perhaps only in physics does the old dream really survive, amongst those (somewhat Spinozist) physicists who think that we are within reach of a complete fundamental science of nature, a unified theory of everything.

In which case how is the dilemma to be resolved? How are we to reconcile the intense attractiveness of the systematic ideal in philosophy and theology with its seeming incoherence and un-attainability?

The answer I propose is that we should see systematicity as an art-ideal. We should dispense with the idea that the world is objectively fully determinate, and that all knowledge is totaliz-able – and indeed is already totalized in God's absolute and per-spectiveless vision. Instead we should see a philosophical text as proposing a group of metaphors and making a number of con-nections that resonate very widely and, in the case of a great text, so widely as to present us with something like an art-image of Everything.[4] The text is thrilling and takes us out of ourselves, insofar as it seems to draw Everything together and make Everything make sense. There is no ready-made or antecedently laid-on unity and meaningfulness of Everything, but a great text like Spinoza's *Ethics* may produce an effect of cosmic unity and meaningfulness that we find liberating and blissful. The text does not describe, but builds a world that satisfies us and makes us feel good. Thus we keep something of what metaphysics was all about: we keep it as art.

In this account, 'Everything' includes 'everyone, including me', and it may even include also 'nothing'. I say this because some of the philosophy that is most attractive today pictures Everything as being so light and transient as to lack any reality of its own. Such an ultralight and minimalist world-picture is apt to be described by those who fear it as nihilism. But it can happen that a nihilist vision of the world evokes a peculiarly intense and objectless wonder, gratitude and love that are profoundly liberating. This brings us to the question of how a religious text can be seen as an art-image of the way to cosmic or eternal happiness.

There is not, for me, any very sharp qualitative difference between philosophical and religious writing. But religious writ-ing does always aim to draw out the subjectivity of the reader

into the Everything that it pictures. In science the subjectivity of
the individual writer and the subjectivity of the individual reader
are left out, so as to allow the scientific attitude to be appropriately disengaged and impartial. In philosophy the subjectivity
of the reader is drawn into contemplating an art-image of
Everything. But in religion the text is meant to function in such a
way as to seduce the subjectivity of the reader out into objectivity. That seduction is religion, and through it the swooning,
feminized reader becomes 'lost in the objectivity of world-love'.[5]
The effect is salvific: one is utterly happy to pass out into a meaningful and unified whole, so that a good religious text frees us
from the fear of loneliness and death.

From this account it will be seen that we accept the 'end of
metaphysics' and with it the (related) end of old-style dogmatic
theology. There is no ready-made or objective truth in either
realm. But we keep both of them as art-forms. It is very important to be able to feel that we can, by the way we live, make some
kind of unified sense of the world and our own place in it. But
none of the sciences delivers this, so there remains a place for
metaphysics simply as art; and that it is indeed art that we are
concerned with here is indicated by the fact that we can and do
appreciate and enjoy imaginatively entering into more than one
of the great metaphysical systems of the past, just as we can enjoy
a wide range of works of art in many different styles without
seeing them as rivalling or contradicting each other.

In our very pluralistic age we can gain great aesthetic pleasure
from more than one philosophical system. We can gain understanding and insight from such a system, and we do not resent its
'closure' – that is, its self-presentation as a complete world – as
amounting to dogmatism; no, rather, we enjoy its closure as
aesthetic polish. And similarly in our post-modern times it is
possible to enter and to gain spiritually from more than one
religion. As I have confessed often enough, when I am in
Christianity I like Christian personalism and the female eroti-
cism of Christian mysticism. And when I am in Buddhism I like
the sublime restful coolness of Buddhist spirituality. The two
traditions are about as different as can be, but after the end of

dogmatic or objective truth they are no longer seen as contradicting each other or as being rival claimants to our allegiance.
Religious exclusivism is nowadays as out of date as nationalism.
It is a joy to be rid of objective truth and of the ugly exclusivism
that always goes with it. There is nowadays no reason why our
own living and world building shouldn't be nourished by many
different influences.

In conclusion, we see systematic 'closure' in aesthetic terms. It
is the artistic polish or finish that rounds off an autonomous
fictioned world of thought and feeling, and gives to it its own
special atmosphere. But the systematic completeness and unity
that I am talking about is not the completeness of a system of
objective knowledge: it is the completeness of a well-imagined,
carefully wrought, widely resonating and seductive work of art.
The work of art, whether it is a philosophy or a religious text or
a work of fine art, represents a possible 'finishing' of the world,
and as such may influence the way we feel about things, interpret
our experience and construct our worlds.

4

Beginning all over

From what has been said so far it will be gathered that I want to be finally rid of the idea that there is any ready-made or object-ive, religious or philosophical truth out there at all. Truth is a property of sentences only, and we do all the talking. The world as such and apart from us is formless and indeterminate. It waits to be finished by the way we describe it and the way we interpret it, by our feeling response to it and the way we build our lives. Gradually, communally, we have evolved and are still reshaping both our finished world and ourselves. Religious and philo-sophical texts are artworks that in condensed and symbolic form propose alternative ways of finishing the world. They recom-mend new ways of seeing things, ways of feeling about things, and attitudes to life. 'Try looking at it this way', they say. Thus they do not give us information, but rather suggest to us alter-native ways in which we may build our worlds and become ourselves.

This is to say that the fictional world created and proffered to us by a philosopher is not so very different in status from the fictional worlds created in modern times by various novelists. And indeed in the twentieth century there have been a number of philosopher–novelists such as Sartre and Iris Murdoch, and also many writers like Samuel Beckett who, without being themselves philosophers, do very much the same job as a philosopher by pre-senting a mixed-media philosophy of life in the whole corpus of their work.

A familiar religious example that makes all the same points is to be found in the fourth gospel, the Gospel of John. The Johannine Christ is clearly not the historical Jesus. The book presents a fictioned cosmic Christ as someone that one can and should live by. He is just such a work of art as I have been describing: Christ pictured as a religious role model around whom one can build one's life. As such he is 'the Way, the Truth and the Life'. To live by him is to do the truth and to abide in the truth. It is evidently all too possible for popular Christianity to read the book metaphysically and to understand it as making – or even as justifying – grand dogmatic claims about Christ. But even the most cursory glance at the ways in which the word 'truth' is used in the Johannine writings indicates that the metaphysical way of reading the text is not the only one, and not the best.[1] In William James's language, John's truth is 'lived-truth' and not 'logic-truth'.[2] He's talking about practical trustworthiness and reliability, and about moral consistency. John is not talking about the objective truth of the church's christological dogmas. There were no creeds in his day, nor any 'New Testament' either. He is not talking about which is the correct theory of the world: he is talking about what we should live by. He does not put speculative truth first: he puts life first and the allegiances that are to shape our life. Christ is truth in the sense of being the one we do best to live by.

It is very difficult now to grasp how habitual, how utterly taken-for-granted is the dogmatic–realist way of reading a book like the Gospel of John, and what a bad mistake – indeed an enormous mistake – it is.[3] It is a mistake that unites people who might otherwise appear to be of opposite opinions. Consider for example an Anglo-Saxon analytical philosopher and, from the same cultural milieu, a conservative evangelical Christian. At first sight, they seem poles apart: neither of them can open his or her mouth without infuriating the other. But on almost everything that is really important they are agreed. They are both realistic. They put knowledge first. For both of them a religion is a creed, a system of tenets. A Christian is a person who holds, gives his/her heart to and acts upon a complex system of supernatural beliefs – roughly, beliefs describing how beings from the supernatural realm have in the past dealt with and interacted with our world, a process of interaction that still continues. To both the philosopher and the Evangelical the question of the truth of these beliefs, thus 'literally' or realistically understood, is the only question about religion that really matters. If they are not objectively or realistically thus true there is nothing at all in religion upon which one need spend any more time.

Twentieth-century Anglo-Saxon philosophy often took a similar view of moral philosophy. When somebody passes judgment on a question of morality, either he/she is stating facts about moral 'absolutes' or he/she is merely expressing feelings of approval or disapproval. So the question about ethics is also made into a question about realism: either you are a moral realist, or you are a mere emotivist and, what's more, you are probably sunk in a morass of 'relativism' as well, so that we need spend no more time talking with you.

How did we get involved in these philistine ways of thinking? Behind analytical philosophy stood the long-standing tradition of positivism. Everything in human thought and experience comes down in the end to facts, and feeling responses to the facts (or alleged facts). So either moral conviction and religious belief have a solid basis in fact, or they are matters of 'mere' feeling, that is, feeling with no real factual basis.

I want to escape from this dilemma. In morality and religion our concern is with what we should value, how we should build our lives and our world, and how we can be happy. The search for truth in morality and religion is not like a search for buried treasure that, one is told, is already sitting out there waiting to be discovered: it is more like a young person's search for a vocation in life, or an artist's search for a distinctive voice and style. You have to find the way of seeing things, the set of values, the life-policy and the dream that's right for you, because through it you can best express yourself, become yourself and find life-satisfaction. 'True' religious beliefs are beliefs that work for you in this way. Thus, a religious seeker is not a person who looks for a set of ready-made objective religious truths, but rather is like a person who looks for a coat that suits him/her – suits him/her so well that we might say, 'That coat is you!'

Why did people ever come to think otherwise? How did it

come to be universally supposed that you cannot be a Christian except upon the basis of believing six impossible things before breakfast? I have in the past suggested that our thinking about religion became very distorted in its struggle to respond to the overwhelmingly great 'truth-event' of the rise of early modern science. In the seventeenth century classical physics suddenly seized power at the cosmological level, and made very strong claims for the dogmatic truth of its own new mechanistic world-picture. To survive, religious thought had to make – or thought it had to make – equally strong claims for itself. As a result, the language of theology came to be understood in a much more 'literalized' and realistic way than previously. The best example of this is the rise during the seventeenth century of 'literal' deism and theism, replacing the more dramatic and symbolic God-talk of earlier ages.[4]

That maybe so, but I fear that a theory along these lines would be hard to demonstrate in detail. A much more persuasive theory of dogmatism points to the very ancient Christian pre-occupation with spiritual power, and its ever-greater concentration in the church hierarchy.

Here's a cruel and unedifying analogy: a lifetime ago, stage hypnotists were adept at picking out the more suggestible members of a music hall or vaudeville audience, and getting them up on the stage. The show that followed entertained and delighted the crowd precisely as a spectacular demonstration of the hypnotist's spiritual power over his willing victims. He proved his power by the utter ease with which he made them say and do ridiculous things. By 'post-hypnotic suggestion' he could implant a command at the unconscious level, so that the victim would remain in his power and continue to obey him even after having woken up.

In those days the audience were seemingly not offended by the systematic humiliation of the hypnotized victims. People just love a display of power, and it was presumably taken for granted that human beings love to be the fascinated and humiliated victims of spiritual power, just as they love to be the almost-equally humiliated victims of the erotic power wielded by some persons and of the political power wielded by those military leaders who are able to march them willingly off to death in war.

And now to apply the analogy: in Christianity the ablest and most dominant men have since very early times tended to subordinate truth to power. They have no doubt cared about religion, but they very firmly subordinated the religious interest to the concern for spiritual power. They thought their duty was to build up the church, and they thought that the way to do this was to increase the spiritual power of the church, which meant and means their own power, the power of the hierarchy over the church. And there is no more dramatic and convincing demonstration of spiritual power than a display of one's ability to induce people willingly to believe six impossible things before breakfast.[5] The minute definition of dogma, the imposition of tests of faith, and the detailed regulation of sexual life all has the purpose of displaying the triumph of the concentration of spiritual power in the hierarchy in general, and in the Papacy in particular. And to tie everything together, God the Father is worshipped for his almighty power, and from the late Middle Ages was depicted in the image of the Pope, wearing the triple tiara. Nor was protestantism very different: western culture came to equate true religion with power-worship, and the test of the authenticity of your power-worship became your readiness to believe all that the master hypnotist commanded you to believe. The more absurd, the better. Even to this day many people still love to see others, and often wish to be themselves, in a state of enthralment to power. We may laugh at extreme erotic enthralment, we may disapprove of political enthralment, and we may sometimes actively try to extricate people from enthralment to a cult leader, but the grandest and most spectacular forms of spiritual enthralment still arouse much respect and envy.

It should not be so, and the ways of thinking that idealize a state of enthralment to power should not be encouraged – certainly not by a philosopher. Since the Enlightenment philosophers have rather been whistleblowers, keen to expose the crude stage machinery by which some people are able to gain and maintain great power over others.

Since our present business is not with ecclesiastical theology but with a branch of philosophy, namely the philosophy of religion, I propose the following tests.

First, we should discount beliefs that are held only because one is enthralled by the person who proposes them for assent and in order to prove one's own loyalty and his spiritual power.[6]

Second, we should also discount beliefs that are held only because they are held. In philosophical eyes, that it is traditional is no sort of justification for any belief.

Third, we should test our current religious beliefs, practices and institutions by a simple thought experiment: 'If all this that we have received were suddenly and completely to vanish from amongst us, exactly how much of it would we feel impelled to reinvent and re-establish because we truly need it?'

And then, fourth, if it should happen that none of our received religious beliefs, institutions and practices passes the tests, then we are in the situation – in the American idiom – of having to 'begin all over' and make a fresh start. This is not an impossible position to be in, by any means: we need only ask ourselves, 'As things are now, and in our present situation, what religious outlook, belief and practices would work effectively and be philosophically satisfactory?'

5

How it is with us

Most books on the philosophy of religion are designedly introductions to the subject. They give the student an outline history
of the subject since Plato, introduce some canonical names, and
trot out the stock arguments for and against the standard list of
topics. Being designed for academic use, the writing has an air of
objectivity about it. The author does not conceal his/her own
views, but neither does he/she develop them in any detail. The
reason for this is that the predominantly historical approach
and the very miscellaneous list of topics leave no room for any
systematic statement of the author's own views: he/she is effectively confined to intelligent crossbench comments and judicious
summings-up. And no more than that, after all, is going to be
expected of the book's readers. Here, as in most of the arts subjects, the modern university does not teach one to be a doer, but
only an historical critic. You don't learn how to philosophize
yourself, or how to be a religious thinker or a poet or a politician.
You don't learn to be a performer; you learn only how to be a
good critic of other people's performances. In the modern university you are carefully trained not to take your own subject too
seriously, because to do so would be embarrassing and dis-
ruptive. The orderly annual routines of the place would be
thrown into chaos. So you are taught to be cool and to remain at
one remove from your subject, dealing with it in a manner that
ensures it is never going to make the slightest difference either to
your own life or to anyone else's.

We are too sophisticated now to be able to cope with big,
simple questions. But suppose that there actually was a university that dared try to teach students to begin at the beginning

and to philosophize about religion for themselves. What would trainee religious thinkers learn to think about?

So far are we from any first-hand intellectual engagement with life, that most people would not have a clue how to answer the question. The answer in fact is that they would learn to think about the human condition. How is it with us human beings? – the question that is pursued in the old mythologies and is still pursued, with pretty much the same syllabus, in a modern book like Heidegger's *Being and Time*.[1]

In the old mythologies the main concern is to understand how we human beings are placed within the whole scheme of things. The cosmic order is sketched and the creation of the first human beings is described, with attention to the development of the self and the relations between the sexes. Human beings are placed morally vis-à-vis gods and spirits on the one hand and animals on the other. There may then be accounts of the moral law, of the end of the Golden Age and of the conditions of life for later generations of human beings. There may also be an account of the origin of death.

In the myths one is aware of the asking of questions such as these. 'How have we come to be here?' 'How is it that, unlike the beasts, we are conscious, language-using creatures – and indeed what is the meaning of the peculiar power of language?' 'In just what manner are we inserted into our world?' 'Why are things not as they might be, and surely should be for us? Did we do something wrong?' 'How are we to live, and what can we hope for?'

These are still very good questions. We would all of us benefit from some training in how to handle them profitably for ourselves. But we won't get it. The most we are likely to get is a chance to write a critical essay about some authoritative critic's discussion of the handling of these questions in some standard text, or in some other culture long ago and far away. Or we may be lucky and get a chance to study the one modern writer, Martin Heidegger, who did make a direct attempt to rethink the human condition. He is evidently following much the same syllabus, but he spends much more time on the peculiarly difficult topic of the

precise manner in which the human self is set or placed within
the world. This means getting clear about embodiment and
action, as well as about I and Me, We and Us. Not easy.

There are other respects in which new knowledge has somewhat revised the old syllabus. Since the Enlightenment there has
been a vast growth of historical knowledge, and a huge development of historical sciences of nature. We now seem to be profoundly interwoven, physically with our natural environment
and culturally with the historical epoch in which we live. It now
appears that we were not placed naked in a ready-made world:
modern philosophy sees us and our world as having shaped, and
as still shaping, each other. But when all this is said and understood, and when the scientific grand narrative of cosmic and
human evolution has been recited, then, *then* the nature of
human selfhood, the manner in which it is inserted into the
world, and the questions of how we can be happy about our own
transient life, and of what we should seek to become – all this
remains as great and mysterious as ever.

Philosophy is for people who remain restless, dissatisfied and
curious even after science has said everything it has to say (which
nowadays is a very great deal). So the old questions about how it
is with us still have a great deal of mileage in them. And when
we have outlined our philosophy of the human condition, we
may find that we are left with a certain unsatisfactoriness or
unhappiness or discomfort that could perhaps be cured by
religious training and religious practice. That question is to be
dealt with later.

Part Two: We and Our World

6

The relation between language and reality

If we are now trying to get started in human philosophy – that is, if we are trying to get clearer about how it is with us – where do we begin? What's the best entry-point, the firmest ground? Should we, for example, start with the I, the individual self, and then work our way out to other selves and the common world about us or might it be better to start with something that is always saner and steadier, namely the social consensus, We? Or might it not be better still to follow the example of scientists and reporters by coming out of the realm of subjectivity and pushing the focus of our whole attention forward into the objective world? It would not be surprising if someone were to argue that the roaring success of science shows that it is much easier to leave out the self and concentrate coolly upon describing and theorizing the common public world. So let's get the world right first, and then consider how to get the We and the I fitted comfortably into it.

It would at this point be worth pausing to spend some time on the triad I, We and Our World, working out the pros and cons of each as a starting point. But first I am going to propose a different triad, which I believe to be philosophically more powerful. It consists of the three central topics around which western philosophy has revolved: *being*, the central topic of ancient philosophy, *human knowledge and consciousness*, the central topic of early modern philosophy and *language* (or 'the sign'), the central topic of contemporary philosophy.[1]

The way into philosophy

Perhaps the oldest and best way into philosophy, perhaps the presocratic way, is through awe and wonder at Being. By this I mean the continual gratuitous outpouring of all existence or, put more simply, the forthcomingness of everything. It is this upon which we should concentrate our attention, but unfortunately our sense of everything's be-ing is usually badly distorted and deformed by the misuse of the question of being in the service of theistic apologetics – bad ontology and bad religion. People ask, for example, why there is anything, rather than nothing – their intention being to set up the existence of any finite thing as a problem to be solved by invoking God. This is bad philosophy and the best answer to the question, 'Why is there something, rather than nothing?' is, 'Why not?' Nobody is ever going to be in the situation in which nothing exists and he/she can congratulate him/herself on having no problem. Being is in one sense perfectly ordinary, and when we are contemplating it we are not contemplating anything that we have reason to call unexpected and puzzling. We are not looking at something that in turn is looking over its shoulder and trying to see its own cause. We are simply attending to everything's easy spontaneous continual silent outpouring. Everything comes forward, and is just there. It's not a problem; there is no difficulty about it. It's just wonderful. I used the word 'gratuitous' earlier to try to catch what seems to be the groundless, reckless generosity of all existence. That is what is awesome. Pure contingency, always pouring out of nowhere for no reason. Easy come, easy go.

Another mistake that needs to be noticed and then set aside is that of mixing up the question of being with the conservation of matter and the persistence of physical objects. People may think, 'Well . . . things are made, and then they lie around until something happens that dissolves or destroys them. We are not filled with awe and wonder at the fact that physical objects remain in being where we left them, are we? On the contrary, we expect them to be still there. So they damned well should be. We would only feel wonder and puzzlement – or perhaps, annoyance – if we were to find that they had disappeared for no good reason.' But this alarmingly common-sense observation misses the point of the question of being. Especially in the last two centuries or so, philosophers thinking about being have been impressed by the thought that everything is contingent, everything is a might-not-have-been; everything is temporal, and therefore transient.[2] Physical objects are only a very small part of reality-as-a-whole (think of the being of songs, sunsets, paradoxes and Tuesdays), and it has long been thought that belief in relatively persistent physical objects must be secondary, because it is obvious that the events going on in our sense organs that give us our evidence for persistent physical objects are very fast changing. The world that is immediately given to us – the world of sense experience and of moving language – is all of it exceedingly transient. It is pouring out and passing away continuously. Being is not the inert remaining-there of a thing; it is a process, like a fountain.

Everything comes, to pass. Everything is temporal, everything is finite, everything is contingent and might well have been otherwise. Nothing has to be: everything just happens . . . to be. If we pause to think, we may recognize that just the continuing to be, or remaining in being, of relatively permanent physical objects is itself also wonderful. Some philosophers have tried to overcome the sense of mystery by saying that it is enough to regard the state of a physical object at t^0 as sufficient reason (other things being equal) for its being found to continue in existence at t^1, and so on. But it seems very odd to regard one state of a thing, or indeed one state of the whole world, as the creator *ex nihilo* of its next stage. And in any case, I am more impressed by the fact that nothing is permanent: buildings, mountains, everything is very slowly crumbling away as one looks at it. On the astronomical scale, everything is transient. On the smaller scale, if you are philosophical enough to be reading this, then you have probably at some time marvelled at your own continuance in being, which you yourself do so little to secure. We ourselves are relatively permanent physical objects, but we don't know how. We don't even know how we come together – or pull ourselves together – as we wake in the morning. It can be traumatic, just trying to come to terms with the radical contingency of one's own existence – so traumatic that I suddenly think that all normal consciousness is false consciousness, busy protecting itself with fictions of stable, reliable self-identity and continuity. Could we live on the basis of a clear acceptance of our own radical contingency, and the gratuitousness (or graciousness) of Being? Could we? What would it be like to live that way?[3]

The second possible starting-point for modern philosophy lies within the world of human knowledge and consciousness. This is the world we are always in, the world of 'Man', the human world that has come to spread itself over and include everything – and a world of which idealist philosophy was more aware than most of us are nowadays. We never see the world, or anything at all, as it is in itself and apart from us; we only ever see anything as it looks in its relation to, and as within, and as lit up by, our human consciousness of it – which means, simply, our human descriptions and interpretations of it. The world of thought is not an inner world: it's the *external* world that 'fills our thoughts' and is filled out by them.

Until the seventeenth century the physical world about us was very under-described and under-theorized. Since Aristotle the total number of biological species recognized had been scarcely more than a thousand; today, it is several million. In the past, people had not the least idea of how even an ordinary, everyday thing like a tree is constructed – how it lives and grows. They knew almost nothing of the causes of things. Where people's ignorance was so profound, it is not surprising that their world was not familiar to them, and they did not see it as being fully their own. On the contrary, many things could be seen, and were seen, as being under the control of gods, spirits, monsters and wild beasts. Human beings only ran a small part of the whole show, and much was mysterious to them.

Today our knowledge has multiplied much more than a thousand-fold. By chemical analysis of core samples drilled from the Arctic and Antarctic ice, we have already largely written climatic history, year by year, for many thousands of years back. Evolutionary history is being written in minute detail, and the entire human genome will very soon be on record. Just within the twentieth century, the number of galaxies has risen from one to one billion, or even one hundred billion (all in principle observable by the Hubble space telescope).

The new knowledge transforms the way we see the world about us. Everything in sight is now minutely described, theorized in great detail, and in many cases is now easily readable historically. Every moderately educated person is already getting into the habit of reading landscape in terms of geological history, farmsteads and fields in terms of the history of agriculture, individual organisms in terms of evolutionary theory, and items in the built environment in terms of architectural history. The result of all this is that almost the entire world has become comprehensively familiarized to us. Our language and our theories have become deeply interwoven with the way we see everything and with the way reality itself is constructed. We have projected ourselves all over and we are now mixed into the world that we see about us.

There are obvious consequences of this. First, the world about us is now so steeped in our language and our theories that we have as good as completely appropriated it and familiarized it to ourselves. We see everything as ours, that is, through the language in which we describe it and the theories in terms of which we understand it, to such an extent that the distinction between facts and interpretations, *the* world and *our* world, has been erased. It's all ours, all interpretation, all the way down. Apart from our input, apart from our language, there is only non-language, which is formless, ineffable Being. Being comes forward and fills out our descriptions rather as gas from a jet fills out a balloon and carries it away.

Second, now, in forming and differentiating the world of experience, language makes everything very clearly focussed, sharp and bright. An indication of this is the unprecedently large number of different hues that the human eye can theoretically distinguish and that industry may be called upon to produce to order – between one and ten million, according to current estimates.[4] This brightening or clarity of the world is the same thing as consciousness, by which I mean that most of our intellectual activity takes place not in our heads, but out there where we are interpreting our perceptions and building our world. This intense world-producing activity is what makes the world as we today perceive it so bright, so full of glory, and it is also what makes our perception of it so vividly conscious.

Third, all these considerations explain something that idealism understood better than we do, namely the fact that 'mind' is communal before it is individual. It was naïve of Genesis to picture Adam as naming everything solo. Just as a market price is determined only within the flow of a continual stream of trans-actions, so linguistic meaning is also transactional. It is held steady by a continual flow of usage. So language and mind generally are social, transactional, interactive, processual. Mind is spread over all the world; mind is a humming web of com-munication within which reality is held steady (or fairly steady). So, when you look at the world about you and are again dazzled by its brightness and its rich, intelligible clarity, remember that the reason why it looks so good is that you see it, not just with your own eyes, but with *our* eyes, the eyes of us all.

In view of all this it would not be at all surprising if the current rapid growth of knowledge, computer power and telecommuni-cations were soon to be accompanied by a revival of Hegel's version of idealism.

The third possible starting-point for philosophy is Language, or 'the sign'. The founder of modern continental philosophy, Kant, argued in great detail that the empirical world about us is formed by the categories and concepts through which we do and must think, so that it can be for us an objective world. But Kant was the last great philosopher whose thinking was consistently governed by Plato's binary contrasts, and very soon after him the focus of philosophical attention was shifting away from Plato's world of 'noumenal' or purely intelligible truth towards the finite, contingent, historically evolving human realm. At the same time, during the nineteenth century modern study of language was getting under way, with scholars writing the histories of words, and attempting to classify natural languages and reconstruct their genealogical relationships. Putting all this together, it is not surprising that Kant's formulation (the world is formed by the categories and concepts through which we think it) came to be replaced in due course by a new doctrine: the world is formed by the language in which we describe and interpret it. Kant called his doctrine transcendental idealism: the new doctrine is liable to be called – often, by its opponents – linguistic idealism, discursive idealism, linguistic naturalism or semiotic materialism.

The shift to this new doctrine is usually accompanied by the claim that we think entirely in language. More exactly, all propositional thought (thinking *that*) is linguistic, all meaningful thought involves general signs and even when we merely entertain a simple image from sense perception, language is still involved in the recalled image, just as it was in the original sense experience.

I have set out elsewhere a detailed set of arguments to show that what is grandly called discursive thought can be re-described without loss as a movement of incompletely executed sentences somewhere in our heads – perhaps just above the soft palate.[5] In what follows I summarize the six main arguments.

First, what could non-linguistic thoughts possibly be? We cannot say what sort of change the conversion of sentences into non-linguistic thoughts might be and, looking at the opposite process, we cannot say how we could ever tell whether certain sentences do or do not accurately convey the non-linguistic thoughts behind them. Is it not obvious that thinking is a way of talking to oneself, and talking is a way of thinking out loud? Is not the 'stream of consciousness' simply a stream of words? When I say, 'A penny for your thoughts', I ask you to utter words, and when I 'read your thoughts' I read them as words.

Second, our being of like mind and able to communicate successfully with each other is much better explained if we put the common language first and treat individual subjectivities as so many privatizations of it than if we begin within one subject, such as myself, and then try to get across to others. If in the manner of Descartes I start within my own subjectivity and have to translate my thoughts and feelings into words, and then transmit them across to you, and wait while you translate them back into thoughts and feelings of your own, if all this must happen every time, how could we ever dare to be sure that we understand each other aright? But if it is true that one and the same language runs through your head and through mine, then the problem vanishes. Our likemindedness is secured by the public character of linguistic meaning. It's wrong to think that each person's mental life is private and mysterious, for the intelligible elements of which it is composed are all of them publicly established meanings. That's why my wife can read me like a book, isn't it?

Third, it has come to be recognized in modern times that every human being is culturally programmed. Nobody's mind is ever a blank slate. We are always within a particular world-view, valuation of life, and set of local customs and prejudices, all of which combine to give us our cultural 'identity'. How did we first pick up all this? We picked it up as we learnt our mother-tongue and all the customs and assumptions that come with it.

Fourth, we think in one natural language or another, and may even be slightly different personalities in different languages. Evidently we do not think in a standard universal language of concepts common to humans and angels, as Dante supposed.

Fifth, the endless running, *perpetuum mobile*, divergent character of thought is exactly like the same feature of language. What's more, when we relax in order to think, we are aware of a furiously rapid scurrying about of rather fragmentary sentences. Thought is a remembering, a rehearsing, a simulation, an entertaining, a play and a letting-rip of language.

Sixth, since Lacan it has been easier to see something that is now very obvious about Freud, namely that his way of investigating the unconscious by examining reports of dreams, association tests, symbolic actions, jokes, double entendres and so on all implies that the unconscious itself works in language and indeed is linguistic all the way down. Freud's work should therefore be seen, not as proposing a lot of far-fetched scientific hypotheses, but as a form of literary criticism, a 'reading' of human personality.

Language and reality

The three central topics around which human philosophy has revolved, we saw, are Being, 'Man' – that is, the world of human knowledge and consciousness – and Language. If we start with Being, we may see philosophy as attempting to give a general account of reality-as-a-whole: perhaps a philosophy of nature, such as was produced by many of the presocratics. If, second, we start with 'Man', we may soon find ourselves moving from Descartes to Hegel: we begin with individual self-consciousness, and the construction and justification of knowledge by the individual, but as human knowledge grows and grows until it encompasses the whole world and as the world-in-knowledge 'brightens' for us in consciousness, so we come to recognize that both knowledge and consciousness are public and communal before they become privatized and individual. A total reconciling vision begins to open up. And third, if we start with Language we will soon find a new and rather different world-picture developing. Language runs everywhere, language has no outside and language never comes to an end. Both the self and the cosmos decline in importance and we become more interested in the rather newly discovered magic world of symbolic meaning.

These are three different starting-points for philosophy and three very different types of cosmology. I have introduced them for a reason: we need to avoid what has come to be called 'foundationalism'. Much of western philosophy, from antiquity to the Enlightenment, tended to assume that it was right to trace all of reality back to a single founding principle or Arche; and this one from which everything is derived was thought to be rational, self-consistent and perfect. But, says anti-foundationalism, what entitles us to assume this founding unity of everything? Nothing does! So by sticking to the triad of Being, Man and Language we seek to avoid begging the question in favour of foundationalism and we defer for the present the question of what kind of cosmology may in the future seem best and why. Are we going to find ourselves thinking of one complex real world, a universe; are we going to seek an ultimate totalization and harmonization of knowledge in 'brightened' consciousness; or are we going to prefer the endlessness and outsidelessness of living language that is revealed by art? We don't know yet. So we rest our philosophy on a tripod rather than a single leg, and we keep open three different ways into and perspectives upon philosophy.

Returning now to our present argument, which was to the effect that all propositional thought (all thinking-*that*) is transacted in a natural language, and that even mental images are language-dependent (in the sense that consciously to see red as red, and to be able in future to recognize it as red, we need the word 'red' from the outset) – if this argument is accepted, what follows?

All thought, we have found, is dependent upon general signs, upon language. Language is only human, historically evolved and transactional. Its 'life' and its effectiveness are linked with its currency – that is, its being current (from Latin *currens*, 'running'). In a natural language everything is interconnected, interwoven and relative. Language is in continual change and can contain no 'absolutes'. We see the world as language formed, language wrapped. Truth and meaning are found only in language. Language penetrates the world and becomes interwoven with it. All our knowledge is already coded into language; we know things by reading them. Very well, so now go back and count up all the reflexive inconsistencies in this present paragraph, because it is itself written in language and therefore the assertions it contains apply to themselves – in many cases with paradoxical effect. For example, is the proposition that language is in continual change and can contain no 'absolutes', itself subject to change or not?

The point being made here recalls something said by Nietzsche. In his *Critique of Pure Reason* Kant had employed reason to criticize reason, which is rather like the familiar practice of calling upon the police to conduct an inquiry into the integrity of their own procedures. Of course they'll find in their own favour: they must! Similarly, an enquiry into language that must itself be carried out in language can scarcely avoid the conclusion that language is endless, language is outsideless and language is itself the world that contains all the world. Because any inquiry into language is unavoidably an internal inquiry, it must end up with extremely 'internalist' conclusions.

It is hardly surprising that some contemporary philosophers, such as Umberto Eco and Josef Simon, have concluded that 'philosophy of the sign' is all that there is left for philosophy to be. While we are in language, we can hope to learn something of how language differentiates the fabulous world of symbolic meaning and how language comes to be used to do one job or another. But as the Ch'an and Zen traditions in East Asian Buddhism have long recognized, insuperable paradoxes immediately attend any attempt to transcend language or to find language's outside or to speak about the relation of language to non-language. The previous sentence is itself reflexively paradoxical, because 'transcend language', 'outside' and 'non-language' are of course themselves items of language. Indeed, we cannot even begin to talk about getting out of language. As the saying goes, 'Don't even think about it!' i.e. about trying to get clear of language. We cannot even begin to talk about the ineffable, as the Ch'an masters recognized when they pointed out the paradox in saying that 'the highest Truth cannot be put into words' ('Oh, yes? Then has something just been said, or not?').

In the present text I am trying to avoid being trapped inside the 'false prison' of language. It isn't a prison, because we never find its walls or come to its limits. But for the sake of the philosophy of religion, I want to keep Being, perhaps under erasure as the non-word B̶e̶i̶n̶g̶, as an object of religious attention. Being is the gratuitousness or graciousness of our purely contingent existence, Being is hap, Being is the forthcomingness of everything, and Be-ing is (sort of) prior to language. And on the other side of language I want to keep something of 'Man', the world of human knowledge and action in which everything becomes articulated, finished and 'brightened' or conscious, because it is here that I shall want to locate religious joy.

But you'll have to wait and see how it all works out.

7

'Discursive idealism' and religious thought

If all our thinking is transacted in language, then we never see the world directly, or intuitively. We couldn't: there's nothing to be seen. All our experience of things is linguistically mediated. The world is always already coded into language; that is, we have made it intelligible to ourselves, and we have made it bright and visible, by seeing it in terms of words. Out on the common at the moment I see a man walking a dog. I don't first see a perfectly intelligible state of affairs and then, subsequently, seek out an appropriate form of words to describe it. No, from the outset I recognize what I see as being a man walking a dog, in those words. I look, and 'a man walking a dog', in those very words, is what I see. That is how the sports commentator in the great days of radio was able to rattle out a description of events much less than a second in arrears. He did not need to pause and find apt words for what he saw; he simply rattled out, in stream-of-consciousness style, the sentences through which he was making sense of what he was seeing as it happened.

Language used in this way bears testimony or witness to events, recounting, recording, describing or registering them for the benefit of people who are not able to be present in person. So completely does language form our experience that people who listen to a good vivid commentator will tell you that he/she makes them able to picture the events just as if they were there themselves. And it all works, I suggest, because it is through the words he/she utters that the commentator *him/herself* is picturing the events that he/she sees. Language sheds the light by which the commentator sees, or better, language sheds the light that makes seeing conscious. (Without language, our seeing would be nothing but the unconscious blindsight of which certain brain-damaged people have been found capable. I do not know a word for 'blind hearing', but everyone knows what it is to have been wakened in the night by a noise that was heard unconsciously and that therefore cannot be remembered.)

On this account, language, *our* language, is all the time finishing the world and making things both visible and intelligible to us even as they happen. We apprehend the world as a great stream of language-formed events that continually pours out and passes away – 'the fountain'. If I see that I am myself part of the fountain that I contemplate, and if I affirm it and commit myself to its rushing waters, then I see that I am myself passing away at exactly the same speed as everything around me – and that everything around me therefore now looks still to me! I am in an eternal present of rushing speed-of-light transience. That is presumably how the fountain comes to be a healing and reconciling symbol both of transience and of the eternal return – in short, of eternal life.

As for the notion that the whole world is all the time being formed and finished by language, it is of course a rediscovery of an ancient religious idea. In pre-philosophical thought a word is an utterance, and your utterance is a winged messenger that you have sent out to do your will. (The messenger is still remembered: he has wings on his heels or his helmet, or he rides a bird.) In mythology the Creator-God is often found to create the world by uttering a series of words of command, and his action is seen as a model for similar human acts of creation. In Polynesia, for example, the creation myth tells that in the beginning there was universal darkness over the primal waters. Gradually, Io, the creator-god, struggles awake. Light appears, and he cries out, 'Ye waters of Tai-Kama, be ye separate. Heavens, be formed!' and so through these powerful cosmogonic words great lines are drawn across the void, and the world comes into being.[1]

Nor is it only the creator-god who creates a new reality by his utterance, for human beings use the same formula in various of their rituals.

> The words by which Io fashioned the universe – that is to say, by which it was implanted and caused to produce a world of light – the same words are used in the ritual for implanting a child in a barren womb. The words by which Io caused light to shine in the darkness are used in the rituals for cheering a gloomy and despondent heart . . . for inspiration in song-composing and many other affairs.[2]

The Polynesian myth describing the world as having been first formed and 'brightened' by language thus provides an exemplary model for all the human performative utterances that are used to put new life into barren wombs, depressed people, blocked song-writers and reluctant warriors.

The same idea that the myth of the creator's powerful word functions as a model for various sorts of human creative utterance is prominent in the Memphite theology of ancient Egypt, probably dating from the late third millennium BC.[3] Here, the supreme God Ptah conceives gods, the cosmos and men in his mind (or 'heart') and brings them all into being by his commanding word (or 'tongue'). By this action Ptah has made the heart and the tongue the ruling powers of the whole body, not only in men, but in all living things. The text – the 'Shabaka Stone', no. 498 in the British Museum – continues as follows.

> Thus it happened that the heart and tongue gained control over every other member of the body, by teaching that he (i.e. Ptah) is in every body and every mouth of all gods, all men, all cattle, all creeping things, and everything that lives, by thinking and commanding everything that he wishes.

And the text goes on to produce what may be considered the first known psychological theory.

> The sight of the eyes, the hearing of the ears, and the smelling the air by the nose, they report to the heart. It is this which

causes every completed (concept) to come forth, and it is the tongue which announces what the heart thinks . . .

The whole text is worth study. What has happened is that dissatisfaction with the relative naïvety of other cosmogonies – such as the one that has the creator Atum sitting on the primaeval hillock and simply masturbating to create the other gods – has led to the production of a new account in which Ptah creates by first thinking and then speaking out. This more psychologized and linguistic account of creation then generates the first really unified theory of the human being as rational agent.

> Thus were made all work and all crafts, the action of the arms, the movement of the legs, and the activity of every member, in conformity with this command which the heart thought, which came forth through the tongue, and which gives value to everything.[4]

After these examples it is scarcely necessary to add that in the Hebrew Bible, and in the many religious traditions indebted to it, the world was from the outset seen as language-formed, as permeated everywhere by the divine Word, as being made of signs and so on.

> The heavens are telling the glory of God;
> And the firmament proclaims his handiwork.
> Day to day pours forth speech,
> And night to night declares knowledge.[5]

That all events are signs, constituents of a 'divine visual language' that addresses us continually, is also the doctrine of the Holy Qur'an and of George Berkeley. As Geoffrey Warnock put it:

> . . . Berkeley took very seriously what we may be tempted to interpret as a kind of metaphor – the idea, in particular, that that of which we have experience is the 'rational discourse' of a 'governing spirit', that every object and every event is an

intelligently-used, intelligible *sign* set before us by the will of an 'infinite mind'. In a sense, his views can be understood as a protest against the scientific, 'corpuscularian' view of the world. The idea that we inhabit a blankly unthinking, 'inert' and 'stupid', universe, and hence that facts are in the end to be merely accepted; that there comes a point at which explanations can no longer be given because it no longer even makes sense to ask for explanations – this idea he not only detested, but genuinely found incomprehensible . . .[6]

Berkeley reckoned that he was refuting materialism and restoring something of the old biblical immediacy of God's address to us in our experience. But he lived before Kant, and did not consider the possibility that it is we ourselves who impart its linguistic character to our experience, and must do so in order to make our world intelligible to ourselves. We are the only makers of meaning. Only words, *our* words, have significance. So, in order to make sense of our experience, we must project language on to it. Because he didn't see this point, Berkeley was too quick to claim that we moderns can recover the old Hebraic vision of the world as God's utterance to us. The position is a little more complicated than that. It is true that in post-modernity we recognize that we do and we must see the world in terms of language. All our experience is linguistically mediated, and we see everything in terms of bane and blessing, theories, purposes, standard descriptions and stories. Our language forms the world, making it finished, intelligible and bright. One begins to see again the value of the more literary cosmologies of pre-scientific times, and to understand how a book can be a portable guide to Everything. The author of the book is also the author of nature, and the story told in the book is an epitome of the whole enacted story of world-history, from creation to the last judgment. Nature and the book, the world and language, hang together.

So in post-modernity there is indeed a certain return of ancient thought. But we are also reminded that things are not exactly the same as they were. It is true that, as soon as we see it, the world is always already coded into language, but it is not so because an eternal creator's voice has formed it. What happens is that *we* see, and are obliged to see, the world in sentences in order to make our experience intelligible to ourselves. *Coeli enarrunt*, the heavens tell stories, but the stories they tell are ours and the language they talk is ours, human language, with human senses and a human viewpoint built into it.

Berkeley didn't see this point, and leaves himself wide open to objections. He knew that God does not have sense organs and doesn't see the world from just one local viewpoint; so what can the colours we see look like to God, and what can the rainbow we see look like to God? And, what's worse for Berkeley, he did not recognize the extent to which our current scientific theory shapes the way we perceive the world, so that he seems stuck with the idea that God will have to present human perceivers with appearances that are consonant with their own locally current scientific theories, however bizarre. Can that be right?

It can't be, and it isn't. The position is that in traditional society there was just one permanently right way of seeing the world, namely the way God had made it and still presented it to us. There was a ready-made fixed cosmos. Human beings were indeed recognized as having some delegated creativity of their own, but in their own world-building and procreative activity they must take God as their role model and copy his exemplary way of world-building. Thus they do his will, and participate in his creative work.

In modern society the situation is quite different. We have no ready-made cosmos with its own correct interpretation already built in. We are ourselves the world-builders, seeing things through, or in terms of, the ways of describing them that are prescribed by our own current theories.

Here is another curious difference between the traditional set-up and our situation in post-modernity. In the traditional world-view God was a discursive idealist, but we had to be realists. God by his own almighty word created the world out of nothing – or, on another account, created the world by calling it into being out of what our forefathers called chaos or the deep, and we might call quantum fluctuations in the vacuum. God thus saw his own creative word call the world into being and sustain it thereafter. God made the world he saw, and human beings then came along as part of God's creation, and took it as given. Indeed, the world hung upon the creative will and word of God from moment to moment, but for us it was real and we lived and acted only within its parameters.

In post-modernity the situation is oddly turned around. It has come to be seen that language is only human, and that 'culture precedes nature'. In effect, the world is now our world, and our world is the great communally evolved way of seeing things that is held within, is sustained by and is slowly developed by the continual humming to-and-fro of our communicative life. Culture is now seen as a great system of signs in motion and as, in effect, doing the work formerly credited to God. Discursive idealism thus becomes secularized or democratized, as people come to recognize that ordinary human language now has the creative power that in the past was ascribed only to the language of God.

Poets and literary critics were amongst the first to grasp this.

> Will kein Gott auf Erdesein,
>   Sind wir selber Götter!

> If there is no God on earth,
>   We ourselves are gods![7]

What are the religious implications of this change? Inevitably, perhaps, most people's reaction is politically influenced. Whether they love it or loathe it, they see the 'dethronement of God' and his replacement by 'Man' in much the same way as they see the concurrent democratic revolutions against absolute monarchy. Conservatives are horrified, because they assume that when people give up the old way of thinking about God religion must abruptly cease, and they go on to argue that democratic political life will always be corrupt and unstable because human life needs to be guided and held steady by an objective absolute authority. On their view, human beings are fitted only for service and not for freedom. But liberals are thrilled, by the very same events viewed under very similar assumptions, arguing that human beings are at last coming of age and will flourish when they escape from the oppressive disciplinary institutions, religious and political, within which they have lived for so long.

The point to note here is that conservatives and liberals tend to share the assumption that equates religion with submission to an absolute monarch – in short, with realism and 'absolutes'. It is an assumption that is very widely held in the West, and is perhaps only now weakening as the influence of Buddhism grows. And in any case, was it ever justified? If it were true we would expect the 'strong' creative poet or artist to be, and to be seen as, a consciously irreligious type, a Lucifer whose sinful pride leads him/her to challenge God. But do we really see great artists in that way – and did they see themselves-at-work in that way? No, surely not.

Again, if the assumption were correct we would expect a developed religious world-view in which everything is the product of, and is unified by, God's creative activity to be very much richer and more beautiful than the patchy cobbled-together cosmology that has been assembled by us human beings since the time of Copernicus. And it is true that, in western Europe, as elsewhere in the world, people do feel a very intense yearning nostalgia for the old sacred cosmology from which we have been exiled by modernity. We indulge our nostalgia by going to church, by reading Dante, by visiting cathedrals and listening to plainsong. But we deceive ourselves. The old cosmology was in some ways symbolically rich, but it was desperately small scale and narrow. Our new man-made visual environment is more highly differentiated and beautiful than theirs by a factor of many thousands. Even the greatest mediaeval cathedral is pathetically mean and barbarous compared with what is freely available to you in a modern university. How many stars had they catalogued? How many species of plant? Recently, I watched avocets, but in the Middle Ages there was no such thing as seeing the avocet. By our standards, they were almost blind. To a person like me, that is a major consideration, but if you disagree, then consider the equally wide disproportion between the moral worlds of the Middle Ages and today.

I am arguing that it is wrong to suppose that the changeover from a God-made and God-governed world to the newer man-made world of 'culture' has to be seen either as marking the end of religion, or as involving a massive loss of value and order. On the contrary, although in liberal democracy both world-view and the moral order are 'only man-made' and are subject to continual renegotiation, they are also enormously larger scale, more differentiated and more beautiful than what we had before.

True, we are nowadays all of us a little like artists. We are aware of the extent to which we ourselves have formed and are still forming what we see. But it can still ravish us, and we can still rationally take up a religious attitude to it. 'And God saw all that he had made, and behold, it was very good.' Nobody would suggest that there is anything absurd or irreligious in God's satisfaction in contemplating his own finished work, so why shouldn't human beings similarly rejoice in what they have made and see their own creative life as a religious vocation? After all, one strand of belief in God as creator always saw it as supplying us with a role model, so why shouldn't we too find life-satisfaction by labouring, each of us, to enrich our own little corner of the human world?

The mobility of the religious object

Discursive idealism (or, if not that, then at least non-realism) is gradually becoming diffused through culture and habitual to us. An example of the way this is happening is the new use of the word 'perception' to mean a perspectival interpretation, a reading of a situation from a particular point of view. Nowadays we can scarcely not be aware of rapid cultural change and of the sheer diversity of local culturally guided perceptions of the world. None of us sees things exactly as they are: every one of us is always inside his or her own particular perspective, or locally evolved way of seeing things.

A consequence of the shift is that the religious object has

become increasingly mobile, elusive and even protean. This is an interesting change, too little discussed.

From early times two sharply contrasting metaphors for the divine have coexisted. One pictures the god as fixed, irremovably enthroned and sedentary. The other pictures the god as in rapid motion, rushing like a tornado and perhaps regularly metamorphosing or changing his appearance.

The fixed god was a 'lord', at the summit of a power-pyramid. If you are in such a position the only place to go is down, so religious language likes to picture the god as enthroned forever and completely secure. He doesn't move a muscle, he doesn't even bat an eyelid and his immobility is a sign of his undislodgeable greatness, power and authority. He is almost the prisoner of his own lofty status.

With the rise of philosophy this immobility of the god was transferred to the God of the philosophers. God was eternal, unchangeable, self-subsistent Being and Pure Act. Because God is already perfect in every respect, there is no room in God for any change at all. He has to be immutable and impassible.

The god of the old metaphysical realism thus seemed relatively clear-cut, because of the way he was locked into his place as the most-real Being, *ens realissimum*, enthroned at the summit of the cosmic power-pyramid. God seemed fairly definite because God was by definition at the top. I remember an Army friend describing a very senior visiting officer as being 'two down from God'. In an army there is a clear-cut hierarchy of degrees of rank; to get to God, simply extrapolate upwards. In some such way as that people even today can think they have a pretty clear idea of what God is supposed to be: the one at the very top.

However, alongside this motionless image of God there has since early times been another and sharply contrasting image, which pictures God as in constant high-speed movement. He is on the march, going to war; he rides on the wings of the wind; he has a winged chariot, or a barge that sails across the sky; his voice is heard in the thunderstorm. A nomadic people might picture their god as marching along at their head in a pillar of cloud by day and a pillar of fire by night.

This more mobile god is seen as being subject to metamorphosis. He appears often, indeed, but not as himself: he appears in a multitude of different guises and disguises. And this is very curious; why take the trouble to appear at all, if you are to appear only in a misleading guise? The answer is perhaps that the god doesn't actually have any being of his own, or any appearance that is proper to him. He can appear only in misleading, oblique and teasing forms. You begin to guess who he is only as he vanishes, and suddenly you realize that you have been had – and if you are a maiden, perhaps in more senses than one.

During the epoch of 'metaphysics', which ran roughly from Plato to Nietzsche, the 'fixed' notion of God was overwhelmingly dominant, and both believers and unbelievers seemed clear that they knew just what God was supposed to be. Certainly it is very uncommon in that entire period to find a writer saying 'I just don't understand talk about God; I can't see what it can possibly mean.' But in the more recent post-metaphysical period the more mobile image of God has returned. There has been a movement away from realistic theism towards a non-realistic understanding of god-talk. The old sacred world has come back down into its secular base and divinity has become scattered, elusive and multiform. There is not a 'centred' or static and self-possessed metaphysical god any more; instead there are many echoes and glimpses of the divine from the corner of one's eye.

In an age that is highly reflective, very well informed and very pluralistic in belief, it is not surprising that all this should be so. It is not surprising to find that we lack a strong and 'centred' metaphysical God, and in place of him have only echoes, glimpses, rumours and splashes of the sacred.[8] But it makes the task of writing a philosophy of religion much more complicated.

8

The sign which denies that it is a sign

As Wittgenstein remarks, words in a language can be compared with the collection of 'men' or 'pieces' that are used in playing a game.[1] The set of pieces is fairly simple in the case of chess, and more complicated in the case of Monopoly. The comparison we are making implies that the meanings of words are like the 'powers' of the various pieces – the ways in which they can be used, and the jobs they can do in playing the game. The comparison also prompts the thought that in order to understand the point or meaning of a particular move, you must first understand the game that is being played – this means both knowing the object of the game and also being able to work out how a particular move may help to achieve it.

This is good and illuminating, for many of our language-games are indeed just that – games. A flirtatious conversation, for example, is game-like in its enjoyable mixture of competition and collusion. But even in that case, it's not just a game. What the sparring interlocutors enjoy playing with is the possibility that their conversation may become more than a game. It might get serious. It mustn't – but it might.

Thus the comparison between words and the way pieces are used in playing games prompts us to wonder about the difference between games that are played just for fun, just for their own sakes, and games that are 'serious', in the sense that something real and important is at stake in them. Are all of our language-games 'groundless', in the sense that the point of playing them is immanent, and becomes apparent simply in the playing of them or is there some background reality that justifies the playing of the game, in which the game is rooted and to which the game refers, so that something big and important and extra-linguistic is at stake for us as we play the game?

Wittgenstein himself would not have liked this last question at all. He was indeed a sort of positivist or immanentist who thought that the point of each game becomes apparent in the playing of each game, and that we should avoid getting involved with big questions about a supposed objective reality-in-general underlying all the games alike. For example, the sense in which numbers 'exist' is given in the doing of mathematics, the sense in which virtues are real is given in the way we talk about our efforts to acquire them and the sense in which God is real, or 'exists', is given in the ways in which we talk to and about God in church. But we must remember that all our talk about reality or existence is contextual; it belongs within one or another language-game. We should avoid the 'platonic' or 'metaphysical' idea that we can jump clear of all the games, frame an 'absolute' or non-relative idea of the real-in-general, and then assign its proper degree of reality to each candidate, whether it's a number, or a moral object or a religious object or whatever.[2] The different sorts of 'existence' are too disparate for us to be able to take them out of their various contexts and line them all up along a single scale, as Plato tried to do.

Wittgenstein's position is sometimes described as philosophical 'quietism'. He wants us to learn to understand our various ways of speaking in context, and for what they are – and then, to leave it at that. 'This language-game is played', as he says, meaning that the game evidently makes a sort of sense and does a job, at least for now, and when it goes stale and ceases to work, perhaps it will gradually cease to be played. *Che sera, sera.* Meanwhile, we should give up the temptation to try to justify our language-games by grounding them in some unseen and greater reality beyond the world of everyday life.

It is obvious enough from this that Wittgenstein thinks we should not seek to justify religious belief and practice by trying to prove the existence of God. On the contrary, we should be content to explain the Roman Catholic Mass (for example) just in terms of what is observably said and done and shown at a celebration of Mass. Some obdurate sceptic may watch the Mass and say, 'Look, none of all this makes any sense at all to me unless you can convince me that there is a great unseen auditor, to whom all these people are talking and for whose benefit the whole performance is being staged. If he is there, it all makes sense and if he's not there, it's all nonsense.' Wittgenstein would not put up with this for a moment; he thought that the 'realist' notion of God, as a huge invisible being whose existence out there needs to be proved, was profoundly wrong.[3] It was idolatrous. It misses the point badly. For Wittgenstein, if we understand how talk about God and the worship of God work, we understand all there is to be understood and no further question arises.

To explain Wittgenstein's position a little further, we should consider some general points about signs and sign-systems and how they work. Take the case of simple arithmetic: there are the various signs and rules for forming expressions, rules of inference and so on. But nowhere within simple arithmetic is there any guarantee of the existence of anything to which all this stuff applies. There doesn't need to be any such guarantee. All you need is the skill of using arithmetic properly when you need it.

Now take the case of a natural language. Words have 'meanings', for words are explained in terms of each other; that is, words have complex 'sideways' relationships with each other that go on from word to word indefinitely. But nowhere in the entire dictionary will you find a word that jumps the gap between language and real extra-linguistic existence. Language, it seems, moves entirely in the world of meaning. The use of language is a social skill, more developed in some people than in others. But language as such cannot tell us how it hooks on to reality. (Indeed, we don't have any idea, quite independent of language, of what 'reality' might be.) And this doesn't matter. There doesn't need to be any point at which the connection between language and reality is guaranteed. All we actually need is the skill of saying the right thing at the right time.

This implies that we can give up ontology altogether. We can give up trying to prove the existence of this or that. We can give up the old ideas of objective existence and of various degrees of existence. We can replace metaphysics with the much clearer and simpler notion of having the skill of finding the right words for the occasion.

So much for Wittgenstein's non-realism. It sounded very attractive for a while, but it hasn't caught on. Its mood is one of a sceptical melancholy conservatism that knows no higher wisdom than what we already have in our historically evolved traditions. The late Ernest Gellner used to make the point by saying that he couldn't forgive Wittgenstein for his belief that there is nothing beyond culture, but the position is if anything even worse than that: in Wittgenstein's religious thought philosophy explains the wisdom of received tradition in a way that leaves no room for either the critical theologian or the prophet or creative religious thinker or the religious reformer to do anything that makes a real difference. I used to love Wittgenstein for his non-realism, for I took him to be saying that there can be true religion without metaphysics. I thought non-realism opened the possibility of religious innovation and creativity, by allowing us to reason that what human beings have made, they can remake. But in fact Wittgenstein's non-realism and quietism are uncomfortably close to defeatism and his thought now begins to look like a blind alley. It doesn't lead anywhere. In philosophy as in the natural sciences the very best ideas are not the ones that seem to finish the subject off and leave little more to be said, but the ones that are the most productive of controversy and new lines of thought. By that test, Wittgenstein now looks as if he is not wearing well. His followers have not been able to add very much to him.

If we are to escape from Wittgenstein's pessimism and quietism, we need to start from the fact that his ideas have also failed to attract the very religious conservatives and traditionalists for whom they might seem tailor-made. Why? Obviously, because religious conservatives remain firm theological realists. Although they – and certainly the Catholics and Orthodox amongst them – are usually very ready to recognize the highly symbolic character of religious language and worship, they remain firmly insistent that there is at least one religious sign that is more than just a sign, namely the sign 'God'. These religious conservatives agree with the unbelievers that an act of public worship cannot be satisfactorily explained purely internally, as if it were like a modernist play that conjures up a small closed autonomous world that exists only during the performance.[4] No, you cannot fully explain the Mass by working your way around from sign to sign in a closed circle, because it contains at least one sign that is not just a sign, a sign that insists on jumping right out of the world of human signs, namely the sign 'God'.

In the older philosophical tradition there were at least two clear indications of the unique status of the word 'God'. One was Anselm's celebrated ontological proof, which argued that, uniquely in the case of 'God', the very meaning of the word makes it a necessary truth that God does actually exist. 'God', the sign, is not just a sign, but also – and analytically – God the signified.[5]

Anselm's remarkable argument has been first killed off by critics and then revived by the next generation, more often than any other of the theistic proofs, which by my own criterion makes it the most important argument about God that anyone has yet produced. It has proved capable of a great variety of interpretations, ranging from Hegel's view that it asserts that 'the rational is the real' and 'the real is the rational', to Karl Barth's non-philosophical interpretation of it ('Don't seek to justify God: God justifies himself').[6] For our present purpose we pick out the reading of the proof as saying that 'God' is a unique sign, the sign that is not just a sign, for it is the master-sign that rules the whole world of signs, founding it, sustaining it and giving it objective reference.

The second traditional indication of the special status of 'God' is its slightly ambiguous grammatical status, somewhere between – or being perhaps both – a common noun and a proper name. On the one hand 'god' is evidently a common noun, a class term, for it is translated from one language to another and not trans-literated. A god is 'a spirit who is worshipped as having power

over nature or human fortunes'. Monotheists hold that, neces-
sarily, there is and can be only one such being and mark the fact
by giving a capital letter to the only God. But by declaring God
unique and capitalizing him they seem to be on the brink of
making God a proper name; Muslims in particular take half a
step further by turning the Arabic phrase for 'the god' (al-'ilah)
into what becomes a proper name, Allah. Here we see the sign
'God' with a curious dual status, enough like other signs to pick
up the general meaning of the word 'god', and sufficiently unlike
other signs to point out of language like a proper name, with a
uniquely mysterious and transcendent referent.

Evidently, theological realism does have a point, for it has long
been recognized that there is something very queer and special
about the word 'God'. But what is it? The theological realist will
reply that his being objectively *real*, apart from and prior to us
and prior to everything else and indeed to all other signs, is somehow analytically part of the very meaning of the word 'God'. So
strongly do theological realists feel this that they are not able
seriously to consider the possibility that the word 'God' may be
just a word and as much part of the language and subject to the
play of language as any other word.

It so happens, however, that there is a very good parallel case
that sheds much light on the matter. It is the case of money and
in particular of the sign 'gold'.[7]

It seems that the cash economy evolved out of earlier barter
economies via the use of tokens to stand for the items bartered.
In early Mesopotamia, if you had ten sheep to sell, you would
send your servant off to the city driving the sheep and carrying a
hollow baked-clay ball containing ten small cubical clay tokens,
each standing for a sheep. The purchaser, breaking the clay ball,
was assured of just how many sheep he was supposed to be
receiving. The same system was used for the servant's return
journey with the goods he had received in exchange for the
sheep. Thus the farmer and the trader in the city protected themselves against fraud.

One commodity that the trader might send back in return for
the ten sheep was gold, and so a certain unit of weight of gold

might come to function both as a generally accepted and durable store of real value and as a measure on a universal scale of degrees of tradable value. This was a very convenient system, but in order to preclude cheating there needed to be some assurance as to the quality of the gold and the weight of each piece. Since the earliest markets were managed by the temples and also guaranteed and protected by the kings, it is not surprising that early coins came to be stamped with the image of the god or the king in order to give people confidence in their authenticity. Thus the original mint was the temple of Juno *Moneta* at Rome, from whose title we also get our word money.

From this background we can see why the sign 'gold' has always had exactly the same ambiguity about it as the word 'God'. It too is a sign that is not just a sign, because it is also the very signified itself. We use the word 'gold' for money, specie, coins, the system of signs of quantity of tradable value, but gold has also been thought of as the most reliable and tangible and objective store of real value itself. Thus gold functions both as a token of value within the money-system, and as objective really existing value, exactly as 'God' is supposed to function both as a word within religious language and as the really existing Being outside religious language, to whom it all refers and whose really-being-there sustains the whole symbolic system.

The point becomes steadily sharper during the modern period, as the use of precious metals for the coinage gives way to the use first of base metals and then of printed paper. This began the long process of 'the dematerialization of money', which has so dramatically accelerated in our own time with the electronic virtualization of money in bank computers.

As money began to become dematerialized, there was felt to be a need to sustain public confidence in it. Unless paper money was backed by gold, people might fear that it was no better than Monopoly money, and the whole economic system would seem to be a mere game. Central banks, and sometimes other banks also, began to guarantee the convertibility of currency into gold at a fixed rate and also to keep sufficient reserves of gold bullion in their vaults to be able to fulfil the guarantee. The real existence of the gold, as a fixed store of 'absolute' value, underpinned the currency – exactly as the real existence of God independent of the realm in which religious signs circulate is believed by theological realists to underpin and sustain the religious economy. The banks don't actually produce and show off their gold, but we take their word for it that the gold is there, just as in the case of God we take the church's word for it that God really is out there.

The last period in which a situation of this kind actually obtained was the period 1944–71. On 22 July 1944 at Bretton Woods, US and European officials agreed to link the world's major currencies to the dollar at fixed exchange rates and the dollar to gold at $35 per ounce. In fact the system of fixed exchange rates soon broke down, and Richard Nixon ended the guaranteed convertibility of dollars into gold on 15 August 1971. In 1973 Reuters established the first money-trading electronic network.

Thus economic realism – the belief that the whole money system has to refer to and be upheld by a fixed store of value out-there in the form of gold bullion – came to an end. Nowadays money itself is just a flux of relativities that shift daily. Gold has become just another traded commodity and some finance ministers are deciding that it is not a good investment and are starting to sell off the old national reserves, which only makes gold fall still further. The old idioms that, for example, called a young woman out to catch a rich man for herself a 'gold-digger' are out of date.

Mark C. Taylor sums up the new situation as follows.

Going off the gold standard is the economic equivalent of the death of God. God functions in religious systems like gold functions in economic systems. God, like gold, is a sign constructed to deny its status as a sign. The function of God and gold is to safeguard the meaning and value of signs by providing a secure referent. When this referent is abandoned, signs are left to float freely. Meaning and value no longer are determined by reference to a transcendental signified but now emerge through the diacritical interplay of freely floating signifiers.[8]

Meaning, value and reality are no longer fixed and eternal things. They are always already coded into the flux of signs. And money? It is now 'circulation itself'.

My account has differed just a little from Mark Taylor's. As I see it, going off the gold standard is the economic equivalent of abandoning the old illusory realistic idea of God. Now we admit the obvious truth that God is simply a sign, just as money is simply a sign or a flow of signs. And religion is surprisingly little affected. Worship goes on without a realist God just as easily as economic exchange goes on without the backing of gold. What's the problem?

9

Being

Until quite recently, questions about 'ontology' or the theory of being were not prominent in English-language philosophy.[1] The one question that was commonly raised was 'Why does anything exist at all?', which was a question about the cause of something or everything's being and not a question that confronted directly the mystery of *how* things are. What is it for anything at all just to be? How does something come to be?

Anglo-Saxon philosophy had little to say about being. We were very consciously post-Cartesian moderns, who preferred to start with the human subject, with experience and the problem of knowledge. Instead of asking in an 'absolute' way, 'What is there? What is it for something to exist?', we tended to ask, 'What immediately presents itself to us? What are the data from which our thinking starts and knowledge is to be built?' If a British empiricist were pressed on the question of being or existence, he/she might answer that it is better to ask, 'What do we have to go on? What do we start with? What is the most reliable basis on which to proceed?' – questions that indicate that the empiricist's real interest is in the foundations of knowledge, rather than in being. Pressed further, he/she might amplify by adding that perhaps something exists if either we can directly acquaint ourselves with it or we can collect evidence and build up some knowledge of it. Thinking about nature and the natural sciences, the empiricist might add, 'Something exists if it belongs to a world, within which it may interact causally with anything else that belongs to that same world. Since the primary world is the world of human experience, I'm inclined to call anything real if I can have some kind of dealings with it.'

These remarks reveal the early modern and Enlightenment interest in reconstructing the world as seen from the point of view of human life and experience. The chief emphasis is not upon being but upon the data of experience and the construction of knowledge, while the observer, the human subject, is rather taken for granted. Radicalizing empiricism, George Berkeley says that 'To be is to be perceived, or to be a perceiver';[2] and revealing its lack of interest in being, Russell treats existence as simply the exemplification of a description – its happening to have application to something. Neither Berkeley nor Russell attempts to think directly about what it is for any finite thing just to be. They do not take time to gaze head-on at the way the present keeps renewing itself and things come to be, remain in being and, in due time, cease to be. Straight philosophical wonder about being as such is not characteristic of British thought. Perhaps people have thought it unprofitable, as when Ayer in a famous radio debate declared that the mere existence of finite things is just a fact, and an unmysterious fact. Why should we expect it to be explicable? Accordingly, British empiricists have preferred to begin within the human self and with questions about perception, the building of knowledge and the situated-ness of things in a world.

However, as I commented earlier, ancient philosophy norm-ally did start with being. There was no special preoccupation with the point of view of the individual human subject. Instead, one sought a general account of reality, asking what main kinds of entity there are, and then going on to ask why things are as they are. Philosophical satisfaction would come when one fully understood the causes of things, and perhaps when one could deduce the whole diversity of reality from a single founding prin-ciple or set of principles. Plato and (to a lesser degree) Aristotle both thought that one might be able to achieve something like a god's-eye-view or absolute knowledge of reality-as-a-whole and that such a vision would bring with it blessedness.

Heavily influenced, at first by Plato and then also by Aristotle, Christian theology shared this outlook. Unlike the 'Indian' kind of religion that is chiefly interested not in knowledge, but in gaining release from unhappiness, Christianity was oriented towards the gaining of beatitude through visionary knowledge of absolute reality. It was therefore strongly 'realistic' and its universe was densely populated with real beings. Following Aristotle, it took the paradigm case of being to be substance, in the sense of unified independent being. Beings are then either substances or attributes, features or dimensions of substances. Substances themselves were divided up according to whether they were infinite or finite, spiritual or material. This yielded a basic Christian metaphysics, with three main kinds of being: (i) there was God, who is infinite spiritual substance; (ii) there were angels, demons and human souls, all of which are immortal, finite spiritual substances; then (iii) there were all the finite material substances that make up the visible created world, including minerals, plants, animals and human bodies. This visible creation, of which as embodied beings we are part, had a rather ambiguous status. On the one hand it was real, a plenum and good – and here one should remember how deeply shocking in early Victorian times was the realization that a great many plant and animal species had already become extinct, for ever. Until then, people had assumed that the great chain of being was complete and would remain complete. But on the other hand, the visible world was from moment to moment dependent upon the creative will of God for its continuance in being. Without God, it would collapse into nothingness. People often fail to remember this point, but it implies that the death of God must mean the immediate end of all things. In theistic thought, finite or contingent being cannot just hang around, remaining in being by itself. Because it is temporal, it can remain in being only by being continuously renewed from moment to moment.

From this we gather that the traditional religious outlook of Jews, Christians and Muslims was indeed strongly realistic – but everything continually depended upon the power of God. That is why during the early modern period (I mean about 1620–1770, from Galileo to the early Kant) people saw it as so important that they should maintain a synthesis of traditional theism with modern physics. A little precariously, perhaps, people maintained the objectivity of scientific knowledge, declared that the mathematical physicist was 'thinking God's thoughts after him', insisted on the compatibility of philosophical theism and the new 'natural philosophy' and so kept God in place.[3] Thus the approaching major crisis was deferred.

Then came Kant, the Romantic movement, German Idealist philosophy – and an earthquake. The period of theological crisis (1780–1845) began. In the thought of Hegel the death of God is cleverly concealed, but in Fichte, Schelling and Schopenhauer it is manifestly taking place. Kant's intense and detailed critique of our knowing faculties effectively ended the old realism and with it the old belief that we humans could – at least in Heaven, if not sooner – attain absolute knowledge and the God's-eye-view of all things whilst yet remaining ourselves, finite and human as we are. It began to be understood that all our knowledge is and has to be human, perspectival and interpretative, and in the following generations all of human thinking was comprehensively brought down into finitude, into time, into what would come to be called 'culture' and into language. Everything was brought down into the flux of human social life in this world, in a way and to an extent that is well brought out by the fact that the novel promptly became the dominant literary form.

Western thought headed in the direction of scepticism and nihilism, but the full dimensions of what had happened became apparent only in the thought of Nietzsche. As has been well said, it took a century for someone to come along who was bright enough to grasp what had happened and it then took another hundred years for the rest of us to catch up with him – which is why Nietzsche declares that the full implications of the death of God will take two centuries to work themselves through.[4] He meant: one century before me and one century after me. But he himself could see that the death of God meant the end of the old ontology, because we had no theory of how there can be finite temporal be-ing in a world without God. And he also saw that the death of God meant the end of belief in purpose out there, the end of moral realism (belief in a ready-made moral order out there), and quite simply the end of belief in a cosmos, a unified, intelligible, ready-made world out there.

That's serious. After Nietzsche it became clear that there would have to be a fresh engagement of western thought with the question of being. The best person to do this would be someone with a good knowledge of the old pre-Cartesian tradition, both ancient and mediaeval. He would be able to see how the question of being stood at the very beginning of Western thought, how it was bottled up first by Plato and Aristotle and then again later in scholastic metaphysics, and how it has been let out of the bottle by Nietzsche's account of the meaning of the death of God.

I am talking about Heidegger, of course. And it is I think already clear that three considerations must be prominent in the rethinking of being.

First, it is necessary to ask what temporal finite being is, after God. Both Plato and then, later, Christian thought were very keen to secure the absolute priority of timeless unchanging Being, as distinct from mere temporal 'Becoming'. But they failed to recognize the uncomfortable tension between their rather timeless ideas of substance and truth and their ideas about causality and time; they did not foresee that we would one day have to ask how, if there is no Eternal Being, does Becoming manage to keep on coming? They simply didn't stick enough with the idea of the forthcoming of being, or as we might say, be-ing. They didn't stick enough with the highly temporal, flowing and insubstantial character of so much that is precious in our life – for example, personalities, music, days, language and feelings. To cope with our new appreciation of the timebound-ness, the precious ephemerality of everything, the paradigm case of a being would have to be shifted from a substance to an event – recognized, we shall see, as part of the interconnected flow of events in a world.

Second, the rethinking of being is deeply affected by the realization that all our thinking is transacted in language – just as are, at present, my writing, this text and your reading.[5] Even as we think about being, we recognize that it presents itself to us already language-wrapped. So we take up again the old early modern questions – What have we? What is there? What are the data? What is forthcoming? What presents itself? – and we answer that what presents itself is a stream of language-formed events that continually pours out and passes away.

Third, these events are interconnected: they are events in a world. A world is an ordered domain within which everything bears some sort of relation to everything else. And the primary world, the world that presents itself at first, is the human life-world.

We may wonder why finite being presents itself already ordered into a world. Might it not have presented itself in a random scatter of quite unrelated events or white noise? How is it that a world presents itself? The answer is that being presents itself already language-formed and that language itself is as one might say 'world-shaped', in such a way that as it moves over everything, appropriating everything and forming everything, it builds a world. The ordered character of the world is thus an objective reflection of the prior order that is in language. We see a world of subjects shaping objects, a world of nouns and adjectives, of verbs and adverbs and prepositions, of past present and future tenses and of active and passive moods.

It is ironical that we should seem to be coming full circle. The death of God marked amongst other things the end of the idea that the empirical world is a realm of perpetual Becoming, sustained only by God's eternal self-existent Being. Traditionally, it was claimed that without a continual exertion of God's will, the created universe would instantly lapse into non-existence. So how have we been able to survive the death of God? Or, less dramatically, how are we to rethink the question of finite being? How are things able to be? How does the whole world of Becoming keep coming? How are we to think the continual gentle forthcoming of Becoming? The irony is that, so far at least, the answer that is emerging sounds like a return into ancient myth, with almighty and life-giving language moving over the dark formless primal chaos, and forming it into the ordered, brightly lit, consciously experienced human life-world.

The same triad keeps returning to haunt the history of western thought: in Genesis, the darkness of the primal waters *plus* the divine word *equals* the brightly lit cosmos. In Greek philosophy, matter *plus* form *equals* the finished finite thing. In Kant, the raw 'manifold of intuition' *plus* concepts *equals* objective knowledge. Today, the forthcoming of B~~e~~ing (crossed out to make it a non-word for what is non-language, prior to language), *plus* the motion of our language *equals* the bright familiar human life-world.

To get a bit clearer about how the motion of language produces the world, we should consider how it produces us, too. We first learnt to talk by being talked to: that is, we first emerged into consciousness of ourselves as individuals, with others, through a motion of language that preceded us and called us out. And similarly, today, we are emerging as 'personalities', or formed as selves, through the play of language, given out and taken in all the time, in which we live. And it is also through language that we know and recognize our own bodies and work out our manner of being in our world.

It is important here to clear up a slight ambiguity in Heideggerian use of the word Being, because a great deal hangs upon it philosophically. It too can be summed up in an equation: the forthcoming of Being *plus* the motion of language *equals* history as being. Sometimes the word being is used for pure unformed contingency, continuously coming forth. We put it 'under erasure' and write it B~~e~~ing, by way of reminding ourselves that it is an extra-linguistic unthing. But at other times the word Being is used of the whole finished-and-still-unfolding order of things, which we might call simply history.

The question is, 'Why allow this ambiguity to arise and to remain?' And the answer is, to try to prevent the representation-alist way of thinking and representationalist questions from arising. Influenced by traditionally understood religious doctrine, many people think of language as being used descriptively to produce a copy or representation of a state of things that is already established out there, fully determinate and intelligible, prior to our language. Where this is so, they tend to think that the way things are, out there and prior to language, must govern what may rightly be said in language. Truth is then understood to be truth to life, the truth of accurate representation.⁶ Things come first and words copy them.

In this chapter, however, we have been talking about the use of language not to copy, but to produce and form reality. Here, finished and language-formed Being is not supposed to be any sort of copy or representation of pre-linguistic Being. There are not two orders, the real plus the re-presentation of it in language: there is only the one way that things are, as they continually come into being and pass away.

The point is vital, because so many people react sharply against post-modern anti-realism, thinking that it repudiates any control of what we say by the way things are out there, independent of us. They begin to suspect us of saying that there is no objective world about us: life's but a dream, and we may talk into existence or conjure up any world we like – and soon we are being accused of every sin in the book. But this suspicion only develops because people are so locked into representationalism and its assumptions.

How can I make this clear? Look at the scene before you now – the view from your window perhaps. Representationalism suggests that there is a double object and a comparison before you. There's the way things are objectively, and there's the way you picture and perhaps describe them to yourself. Line up the real objects out there with your subjective representation of them, make the comparison between the two, check you've got it right – and now you are in a position to announce triumphantly that you do see the holly bush in your back garden.

I am saying that this whole representationalist way of setting up the situation is absurd. It arose in the seventeenth century at a time when people were trying to reconcile the traditional religious picture of a fully determinate ready-made cosmos with the new Enlightenment way of thinking that had us looking out of our own heads and trying to construct our own picture of the world. Hence representationalism: we were trying to make our own human and subjective world-picture into a good copy of the old God-made cosmos, antecedently laid on for us and still (as we thought) surviving out there. But it is absurd that we should still be thinking in such ways today. I look out of the window and I don't see two things, namely a ready-made real world and my own mental representation of it, for I see only one thing, the world, my world, Being continuously renewing itself, fully formed by language and bright with my consciousness of it. There's only that one reality and the old dualisms, between matter and mind, between objective reality out there and my subjective representation of it, between *the* world and *my* world – all those binary oppositions are dead.[7] They no longer do any useful work. There aren't two worlds, the world out there and the world in my head: there's only one world. It's so much easier and more straightforward when we slough off the old, dead way of thinking.

We return now to the question of being. What is finite being, how does it emerge, and how does it keep continually renewing itself? Since Being as such, prior to and independent of language, is ineffable, we cannot look at it or speak about it directly. But I find that something can be learnt from three analogies of it and from one indirect approach to it.

The first of the analogies is one long familiar in poetry and mythology, which compares the coming to be of every thing with the emergence and formation of new life in the mysterious dark maternal void of the womb – perhaps, the womb of time. As the new being becomes fully formed it emerges into the light of common day and immediately enters the world of language as the traditional cry goes up, 'It's a girl/a boy!' and it cries out.

The idea of woman as a dark, generative void also echoes in the second analogy, from modern physics.[8] Contrary to the old maxim, *ex nihilo nihil fit* ('nothing can come from nothing', often used as a premise in an argument for theism), it seems that there is no absolute vacuum in nature. Even at absolute zero, particles are not simply stationary. Their being so would violate Heisenberg's uncertainty principle. So, even at absolute zero in a vacuum, there is still a certain amount of jiggling about as particles pop into being and pop out again and so on. Thus it seems that the baseline of existence is not a pure nihil, but a matrix of trembling possibilities and micro-events. We may picture it as something like the surface of a pond in heavy rain and describe it as 'the deep' over which the fertilizing word moves.

The third analogy is also from physics, and reflects the effect on my imagination of a combination of Dante's mystic rose from the end of the *Paradiso* with Spinoza's circular vision of a self-subsistent God or nature.[9] Imagine a flat figure made of two circles which touch at a point, as shown below.

Figure 9.1

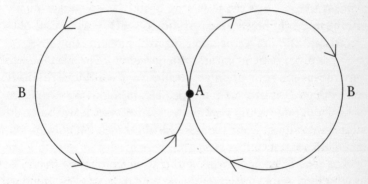

Now rotate the figure through 180° to produce a solid torus, shaped like a doughnut whose hole just closes. Then the point of contact (A) is the initial singularity at the big bang. From it the cosmos flows out over the surface of the torus like a streaming fountain, pouring out until the universe reaches its point of maxim expansion at (B,B). Then the stream of events begins to turn back again, and ultimately returns into the point from which it arose. The energy expended in the expansion phase of the universe is exactly balanced by the energy recovered in the contraction phase. Then we add in the idea bruited about in some recent cosmological speculation that, as Augustine said, being and time are coeval and that from the point of view of the universe all times co-exist – and we suddenly get a striking result. We see that the universe in every part of it might be nothing but

a flux of indeterminate contingency, flitting away, but it may
nevertheless add up to a whole that is self-existent and self-
explanatory.

I must emphasize that these three analogies are only that, just
analogies or philosophical myths. The idea that at the limits of
thought it is permissible and even advantageous to drop into the
language of myth is as old as Plato. Provided that one makes it
clear what one is doing, no harm is done.

As for the indirect approach to Be-ing, it arises as follows. I
have attempted to practise 'moving-edge meditation' by trying to
stop thinking and attend quietly to some gently moving natural
phenomenon, such as the flowering head of a tall grass, quietly
bobbing in a light breeze. I was trying to practise what Catholics
used to call 'the prayer of quiet regard', but directing my gaze
simply at a contingent natural phenomenon. The idea was to
undo the usual rush of interpretation and coolly and still-ly
watch the process of Becoming (or Be[com]ing). I want to learn
to live with and love the very lightness of Be-ing. It was interesting and refreshing – but I was suddenly struck by the thought
that I didn't know and couldn't tell whether I was watching the
self-renewing of Being or whether I was watching time pass. The
thought thus struck me that Being and temporality are one,
which may be why Augustine described them as coeval.

What then is Being? It is the forthcoming of everything.
Everything is finite, contingent, temporal and fleeting, becoming
itself as it comes out into expression, gets formed by language
and passes away. And we? We are parts of it all. Like everything
else, we are nothing in ourselves. We become ourselves only in
committing ourselves to expression and passing away.

There is nothing to regret.

10

The web of communication

It has happened several times in the West since the end of the Middle Ages. First, new technologies or social changes appear to open up a new world of thought and communication. It's often described metaphorically as a new 'space'. Second, enthusiasts for the new space or world locate in it the criteria for truth and even reality. This gives a hint that a rival power is emerging to challenge established authority, so third, traditionalists spring to the defence of the old order, which they declare to be far more 'objective' and trustworthy. As for the new space – the 'inner space' of the mind, cyberspace or whatever – it is, they say, arbitrary and dreamlike. It lacks substance. Nevertheless, and fourth, some radical is sure to come along and declare that it is unnecessarily confusing to have two rival, and very different, regimes of truth with their respective seats in different spaces. It makes life unnecessarily complicated. So the radical attempts to abolish the old world outright, on the grounds that it has now ceased to do any useful job. Fifth, he/she is inevitably greeted with a storm of indignation and ridiculed as a fantasist, but the change he/she was advocating quietly begins to happen anyway. And now, finally, as you and I begin to grasp this recurrent pattern, we recognize that since the end of the Middle Ages the authorities have always understood that the criteria of truth and reality will always tend to be located in the central market – which means in the busiest centre of exchange and communication – so that the question of how that place is characterized, who has access to it and who (if anyone) controls it, is vitally important to their very survival. It is not surprising that the authorities always perceive new communications technologies –

print, telephone, radio, film, the Internet – as potential threats, warn of their dangers and seek to control them.

There have been about five of these new worlds or spaces. The first is the Republic of Letters, an idea that flourished most in the sixteenth and seventeenth centuries.[1] The printed word could disseminate ideas rapidly across national frontiers, linking together not only individual thinkers, but also the many salons, societies and academies that met in cities across western Europe. Gradually, the international consensus of learned people began to emerge as a new criterion and regime of truth, especially in matters of 'natural philosophy' or science. From that modest root has grown all the vast power and scope of science today.

The second new space is the space of individual subjective experience, or 'private judgment', or the 'inner life', first opened up or even (as perhaps we should say) created by writers as various as Luther, Shakespeare, Descartes and Locke. Just as 'the international consensus of learned people' has a theological background in the old consent of the faithful (*consensus fidelium*), so the appeal to subjective experience has a theological background in the mystical tradition. It is hard today to imagine just how weird and weak the appeal to personal experience in the inner space of subjectivity once seemed to be, to people who wielded the immense public and objective authority of the church.

The third new space is the space of the general will, public opinion, 'pressure' and secular democratic politics, emerging in the late eighteenth and early nineteenth centuries and, linked with it, the space of Geist: culture, the climate of opinion, 'the times' and what they require of us, 'the leading edge' of 'where it's at' and history. This space is still bitterly fought over; if you are a young artist, you simply cannot afford not to be where it's at, in the capital city, and if you are a political conservative, you cannot but ridicule every sort of 'trendiness'. But the fact is that the leading institutions in our kind of society cannot be run successfully except by people who are highly sensitive to where it's at, what it's all about and what's going on in this particular space, the space of public opinion and taste.

The fourth new space is the mediascape,[2] the imaginary world of stars and celebrities, conjured up by the news and entertainment media, now playing a very large part in the imaginative life of ordinary people everywhere. It appears to be a new, more secular version of the old supernatural world of religion and to have a similar social function. Celebrities act out our myths, serve as role models and endorse new ideas and values.

Finally, the fifth of these new spaces – and in a strange way, the hungriest of them all – is cyberspace. It is reported on the day I write that a banking transaction now costs £1.70 if it takes place at a counter in a high street branch, but only £0.13 if it takes place on the Internet – one indication of why not only cash, banking and finance, but also a whole vast range of other commercial and cultural activities and institutions are currently being very rapidly 'virtualized'. They are being transferred into cyberspace. Already some enthusiasts are beginning to map cyberspace and are even describing it as being literally the world to come, because they truly hope for virtual immortality for themselves in the computers of the far future. No doubt the time is near when some radical will attempt to overcome, and even invert, our present real/virtual distinction.

I've picked out five new spaces. Others might be mentioned, such as Teilhard de Chardin's 'noösphere', an envelope of humming communication flying back and forth that encircles the whole terrestrial globe. His formulation coincided with the great days of radio. Today, I have suggested, the noösphere has divided into two distinct territories, the mediascape and cyberspace.

The five spaces I have described are those of:

1 the academic 'we': the international consensus of one's peers;
2 subjectivity, the *forum internum* of conscience since late Antiquity, the realm in which, in Protestant Christianity, the Holy Spirit testifies to us inwardly, and since the seventeenth century the space of sense-experience to which the new Experimental Philosophy (i.e. natural science) appeals;
3 public opinion, the verdict of the people, the current trend to

which politicians, shopkeepers and everyone who has something to sell, or who seeks popular support, must pay close
attention;

4 the mediascape, the world of stars, celebrities and role models;
5 cyberspace, the virtual world.

Now, exactly why have we since 1500 or so put such a huge
amount of collective effort into opening up and developing these
new spaces? We should first observe that in some ways they
resemble three much more ancient public spaces, namely the
lawcourt, the theatre and the market, which have been used
since the beginnings of civilization to test out reasons and arguments, to settle claims and achieve consensus, to model the
world and explore myths and to test and stabilize exchange
values, respectively. What happened was that at the end of the
Middle Ages there began in western Europe a process of
explosively rapid growth and social change that continues to
this day. The circulation of printed matter, the voyages of
exploration, the rediscovery of classical culture, the break-up of
the mediaeval Latin Church, the growth of secular cultural life
– these and other factors involved (as they still involve) a great
expansion of communication and a proliferation of new discourses.

A feeling of dislocation eventually developed. People complained it was no longer possible for even the most energetic
and gifted individual to feel fully in command of his own culture.
The individual cannot be testing everything, all the time; it is
impossible to single out and follow every strand of conversation
that is going on in a crowded and noisy room. What was worse,
the mechanization of cosmology after Descartes introduced a
permanent fissure between the world order and the moral order
that has never been satisfactorily healed. In some respects, things
appear to have fallen apart irreversibly – at least in the sense that
a world-view of the old type cannot now be restored.

In the older culture, confidence that one can make a unified,
coherent overall sense of the human condition was expressed by
the general acceptance of the absolute monarchy of God at the

cosmic level and of the king at the social level. But as the notion of an absolute monarch, in whom everything is founded and unified and by whom everything is guided towards its proper end in him, began to break down, people became aware of an acute need to find other ways of coping with the cultural cacophony. The consensus of learned men in the Republic of Letters offered a new and flexible way of validating knowledge; Descartes and a long line of 'I-philosophers' sought to help the individual to find and apply new criteria of truth and to build an adequate world-picture, all within the sphere of individual subjectivity. In social and political matters people learnt gradually to look less to an absolute monarch as the source of authority and legitimation, and instead learnt to look to the verdict of the public; in matters of personal morality, values, lifestyle and myth, people began to look less to the old ideal world of religion, and more to the new ideal world of fictions, stars and celebrities, the mediascape, as the realm in which they see ideal versions of themselves trying out lifestyles, exploring myths and pioneering new values. Finally, cyberspace gives the individual with access to it a vastly increased ability to store, retrieve and process information at very high speed.

There are some obvious and, as yet, unsolved conflicts within and amongst these five new spaces. There is potential conflict, for example, between the third and the fifth of them: between democratic ideas of popular sovereignty and national self-determination, and cyberspace, which is supranational, is already developing its own currencies and perhaps threatens in the end to subvert national governments. Another (and unresolved) conflict concerns the seat of authority: is our most authoritative guide to be the individual conscience (2), the scientific consensus (1) or public opinion (3)?

Setting aside these disputes for the present, it is clear that from around the year 1500 emergent modernity was plagued by doubts about its own legitimacy. How could any humanly con-structed cosmology or moral order be an adequate substitute for what had been lost? How could the Englishmen who in 1649 had legally murdered their own king, the Lord's Anointed, suppose themselves morally competent to create a legitimate form of government to replace what they had torn down?

During the period AD 1500–2000 western Europe continued to be haunted by these questions and failed either to find any lastingly satisfactory answer to them or escape from them. It fell into slow decline, whereas the United States, unique in being an historically and humanly founded nation, has none of our regrets about a half-mythical lost mediaeval period and no sense of sin. It does not know many of the questions that haunt Europeans. It is itself the New World, the Kingdom of God on Earth and a light to the nations. Hence the extraordinary confidence of Americans in their own country – a confidence shared even by minorities and the poor – which has enabled it to emerge during the twentieth century as far and away the world's leading country.

This historical background may help to explain the philosophical ideas now to be presented. In the first place, giving up 'metaphysics' means, among other things, giving up all ideas of transcendent and authoritative validation of our meanings, our truths and our values. No monarch is needed, and no academy is needed. All our meanings, all of our truths and all our values are generated, clarified and maintained only within the continually humming web of our communication. No external validation is needed, none whatever. Even in the case of animal communication it is clear that the individual has a very strong biological interest both in making itself plain, and in correctly interpreting the signals given off by the other. Nobody supposes that animal signs need any external validation. They are used because they work, and we the human observers have in many cases learnt to read them and can easily see for ourselves how they work. The same is true of human signs. We are the most communicative of all animals, with an intense need to make ourselves understood and with an equally intense need to understand others. So we have evolved communication codes that just in their daily use are continually being polished and modified. We greatly admire and seek to emulate those who have the most developed linguistic skills – writers, politicians, humorists, poets and others – so that as its vocabulary and its flexibility have grown, the English language has become the most complex and beautiful of all human creations.

I am espousing thoroughgoing interactionism: all meanings, truths and values are produced, clarified and held only within the web of our communication and the freer and richer that communication becomes, the better. We should support free speech, free enterprise and free trade, rejecting the traditional European leftwing intellectual's attempt to separate symbolic exchange from economic exchange. This is wrong. Economic exchange also involves the exchange of signs and is also integral to cultural life. Industry is culture, buying and selling is culture and don't let anyone persuade you otherwise. There is no justification whatever for supposing that you can combine cultural freedom with a command economy.

Another consequence of thoroughgoing interactionism is that we regard nets as being stronger than chains or pyramids; that is, we see a democratic network as being a stronger social form than the hierarchical kind of organization that is only as good as the people at the top. This has cultural implications, too, and I am now inclined to agree with Wittgenstein that (in cinema) American populism and box-office values visibly produce bigger and more durable art than European elitism.

We can now return to the question proposed at the beginning of this chapter and suggest an answer. The problem was that westerners – or at least, we Europeans – are troubled by nostalgia for the lost sacred unities of mediaeval culture. We feel that we are wandering in the wilderness, exiled from a lost paradise. As our knowledge has grown too great for the individual to cope with, our world-picture has become painfully fissured. We just can't get it all together again. The five 'spaces' that I described were developed by way of helping us to model the world and to cope with our difficulties, but they cannot solve them entirely. We are still stuck with the problem of far too much knowledge, of doubtful quality and status and even more doubtful coherence. We don't seem able to get our world together in a religiously satisfactory way.

In reply I urge that we should simply give up our disabling

nostalgia for a cosmos and a cosy, unified sacred world-picture. No such thing is to be had, and we should be sceptical of terms like 'the Universe', which seem to suggest that it is. Instead we should see the world, our immediate milieu, as a communications network of continuous humming symbolic exchange.[3] Within the flow of its activity, the world itself appears as an outpouring many-stranded stream of language-formed events. The supposed world-order is simply the objective reflection of the order of our language.

Try again: the world is generated by, held within and sustained by our own endlessly humming conversation. We don't need the old sort of ready-made unified sacred cosmos out there: what we've got is real enough for us. The humming conversation of humanity gives us, on its inner face, our selves and our own subjective feeling of our part in it all, and on its outer face religious joy in the world's brightness, of which our own consciousness, spread over our bit of the world, is part.

11

We

One good reason for doing philosophy is that there are some ideas that everybody immediately and instinctively seems to get totally wrong. Why this should be so is hard to say, but it happens and it happens especially with our ideas about language, the self, the mind and time.

Consider this: in one of the very few passages of the Bible that everyone knows, the Earth is without form and void and darkness is over the face of the deep. 'And God said, Let there be light.'[1] Strangely, countless millions of people hear these words without ever noticing that they don't make any sense at all. At the moment when God speaks language doesn't exist and there is nobody about for whom what God utters is language, rather than just a wordless shout. There is no community of speakers for whom what God cries out amounts to an imperative, a command that requires something to happen. To put it bluntly, how does God know what to say? And how can he ensure that what he utters is meaningful language, with a certain force?

Language has to evolve gradually, in a community of persons, but at the moment of God's utterance none of the conditions for the existence of language is fulfilled. He can't know what he's doing and what he does cannot have the force of language. And there is worse to come, for none of the conditions for the existence of a conscious person, who is a speaker and an agent, is fulfilled either. You can only be conscious by recognizing yourself as one of a We created by language and you need to refer to established social conventions in order to describe a bit of human behaviour as an action, as distinct from mere reflex twitchings and meaningless gesticulations.

Thus the idea of a purely autonomous and solitary person, who is conscious, a speaker and an agent all by himself in eternity, makes no sense. And if the book of Genesis makes a mess of God, it makes an equal mess of Adam, 'the man'. Adam is created as a ready-made, grown-up, conscious person. But without a personal history, how can he be a self? How can he know what he is or what his own feelings are? (See also chapter 18.)

God speaks to Adam (Genesis 2.16) and the tradition has assumed that language was indeed taught to humans by God. This cannot be so, because language is steeped in references to space and time and to human bodiliness, sense organs, gender, emotions and so on; the more we consider this the more clearly we grasp that our language is as specifically human as our own bodies are. No non-human being can have taught us our language; we must have evolved it amongst ourselves. But now, note what comes next: God creates all the beasts, and parades them before Adam, 'and whatever the man called every living creature, that was its name' (2.19). The question here is this: Adam is still the only human being, for Eve has not yet been created. So when Adam names one of the beasts, how does the name stick? Normally, when we say 'that's its name', we mean 'that's what it's called', 'that's what they call it' or 'that's what it's known as' – referring to the established custom amongst a group of people. But in this case there are no other people yet. So there is nobody to hear and remember that such-and-such a beast is henceforth to be described by everyone as a camel. So, as earlier, the conditions for saying 'that was its name' are not fulfilled and, again, the story is meaningless.

Now you may protest that these two examples, of God and Adam, are drawn from an ancient, pre-scientific and even pre-philosophical myth. But similar assumptions still pervade the thinking of Réné Descartes, the founder of modern philosophy. For Descartes the human 'I' is self-founding, transparent to itself, centred in itself, self-possessed and autonomous – in short, very much like what God was supposed to be in philosophical theism. And this metaphysical individualism continued to be very popular long after the time of Descartes amongst certain romantics, idealists and existentialists. It is not quite dead yet, for in our own time it is still appealed to by those who take the side of freedom and individual human rights against totalitarian collectivism and corporatism. For example, Evgeny Zamiatin's novel title *We*[2] implicitly takes the side of the individual against the prospect of a world in which the We has become so dominant that people have numbers instead of personal names.

In recent years individualism has also been appealed to by feminists battling to escape the traditional subjection of women and trying to help each other to become more free, independent and assertive without feeling guilty about it. One cannot but feel much sympathy for this struggle, and indeed it is obvious to all that 'the new woman', a capable and confident professional, is the single most original and striking moral creation of modern western culture. But in the long run, and at the philosophical level, the point stands: there cannot be a solitary, autonomous and self-sufficient person. You can emerge as a person only within an already-existing network of social conventions and social relations. Your 'personality' or 'character' is not an essence, but simply a way of describing you on the basis of your comportment in your social relations. In effect, to be somebody you have to have a life-history, you have to be in language and you must be part of a We. You cannot even think unless you are in language, you cannot function as a person unless you have a life-history and an emotional life and you cannot be an agent unless you are 'situated' in a cultural context that supplies you with a range of possible forms of action.

From what has been said it is clear that the We precedes the I. I emerge as part of a We, identifying myself not introspectively, but through what I am in the eyes of others. The self is 'heterological' in the sense that I first get an idea of myself 'accusatively', as a Me rather than as an I. This is very noticeable in young children, whose earliest reference to themselves is markedly accusative. The child prefers to say 'Me' rather than 'I' and even goes so far as to speak of itself in the third person, as 'Polly' rather than as 'I'. The self-defined, autonomous I that thinks its own thoughts, makes its own decisions and lives its own life is a late product and for much of the time we are not too bothered about it. Often we are at our best when we are not concerned about it at all. It is certainly quite wrong to suppose that the real self, the self whose fate matters, is the I, for everyone knows that when we become intensely interested in something or when we are absorbed in love or work – especially creative work – the 'I' vanishes without trace.

Not only does the We precede the I, but also – and even more importantly – the public precedes the private. The public realm is the common space between persons across which language moves to and fro, nonstop. That makes it a bit like 'international waters' in law and also brings it close to the sacred, because historically in each settled community the two premier public spaces were always side by side: one was the forum, agora or market, the place of public assembly, exchange, trial and debate and the other was the sanctuary, the most public space of all. And this public space between persons is more than just a neutral zone or a no-man's-land, because it is the space in which all linguistic meaning, all truth and all values are established. It is everything to us. We live by it all the time. Hence my one-time slogan that 'We live along the wires', becoming ourselves in and through our various exchanges with others – exchanges that are always mediated and supported by the public realm in which they take place. So important is this point that one may say that public space occupies in modern culture the position that God used to occupy – and in Islam perhaps still does occupy.[3]

The We, then, is not just a settled group of persons, but also the public space around and between them, in which their common life is set. It is symbolized and invoked by the formalities that surround government, the lawcourt and the church. It makes every sovereign human community something much more and greater than the sum of the individuals who compose it and it has always been thought to give public officials the right to exercise the power of life and death over individuals.

Is the We intrinsically democratic and egalitarian? This is not a straightforward matter. On the one hand everyone has equal access to language and equal access to the public realm. Even in very unequal societies, everyone is said to be equal before the law, and is usually also reckoned to be equal before God and in death. It seems therefore that in several respects language and the public realm are 'structurally' tilted towards equality. On the other hand, as we have said, the I is relatively late and secondary and for much of the time many, many people simply do not think about themselves or about equality. They are too absorbed in their own business. As it can happen that I can greatly enjoy something without pausing to consider whether I or someone else made it, so it can happen that we are taken up into the constant flux and reflux of language without bothering too much about who's doing the talking.

There is more. Like other biological organisms, we are pushy. We push and shove and compete for the available resources and attention. Every utterance has some degree of force and people differ greatly in their strength and articulacy. So we tend to create inequality. But, against this background, language may be seen as resembling the symbolic behaviour of many animals. It reduces conflict by substituting an exchange of signs for an exchange of blows. It provides a ritual substitute for conflict and, going further, in many areas of life linguistic exchange provides a quick and thrifty way for us to come to an understanding, so that we can say to each other, 'I know who you are, where you are coming from, what you are getting at and what you want. I can tell, I understand.'

Language provides us with a communication code, not unlike animal codes, in which complex social beings like us can quickly come to an understanding with each other. This may very usefully save time, avoid conflict, enlist support and so on. It stabilizes linguistic meanings, for it is greatly to our mutual advantage that we come to a clear mutual understanding with no remaining points of misunderstanding between us. But it may also have the effect of making some inequalities seem more tolerable than they should be.

I make these minor points in order to reach something much more important, which has not been adequately recognized, either in the history of philosophy or in our dictionaries. The word 'understanding' has two meanings. One of them is the classical philosophical meaning of *intellectus* – I understand something when I see it as exemplifying a universal, I recognize it as falling under a general concept or rule, I recognize a logical relation, I recognize a sign that I am familiar with and know how to use. But this traditional intellectual understanding is in real life always bound up with understanding in another sense – that of sympathy, collusion and (nowadays) 'emotional intelligence'. 'I know, I can tell,' says the English person, nodding sagely, but the American is better and more explicit, saying, 'I feel your pain.' That is how the We works: it creates not just linguistic and behavioural attunement, but also emotional attunement. This is a point that our very masculine philosophical tradition has tended not to recognize.

12

I: the first person singular

For many years I took the 'I' very seriously. I was after all raised in the western Christian tradition, the tradition shaped especially by Paul and Augustine and further developed by Luther and Calvin. Then in the 1950s, when a philosophical tradition called 'Existentialism' was rather suddenly invented and popularized, I was much affected first by the younger Sartre and then by Bultmann and – for twenty years – by Kierkegaard.[1]

This latter tradition took to the limit the old western doctrine that one's first concern should be for the eternal salvation of one's own soul.[2] It was a high-anxiety tradition, super self-conscious and intensely concerned about personal integrity and the authenticity of one's own existence. The 'I' was not a traditional platonic sort of self, an immortal spiritual substance, but (in Kierkegaard's words) 'a becoming'. Our life-task was the task of forging or becoming authentic selves, before God and by the grace of God.

Especially in Kierkegaard's version, Christian Existentialism was ultra-protestant. The idea was to translate Christianity as a whole religious civilization, the Middle Ages, into Christianity as a personal faith by which the individual could live in an increasingly secular and post-Christian culture. To that end it was necessary to privatize and internalize Christianity within the individual human subject. The 'screen' on which Christianity was projected was no longer to be the entire cosmos, but simply the individual's self-understanding and life-aim. This meant fitting rather more than a quart into a pint pot; the whole cosmic salvation-drama of classical Christianity had to be contracted down into a psychodrama and squeezed into the narrow compass of the individual subject and his infinite 'interest' in his own existence. The result was inevitably an excessively inflamed and over-violent subjective life, but the believer was supposed to go into the turmoil in faith, believing that there would be personal resurrection on the far side of all the travail.

There are obvious objections to all this. Do we all want to be anguished late-romantics like Franz Kafka? Can it be right to draw such a sharp contrast between one's inner life and one's outward life as Kierkegaard does? Is not the serious Christian who follows Kierkegaard's path in acute danger of driving himself to breakdown? Kierkegaard himself has many moments when he laments his own damaged psychology. He is tempted by the thought that real faith is not to live in a state of permanent psychological crisis, but to return into ordinariness by (for example) marrying Regine and settling for a quiet but worthy life in a country parish.[3]

By the mid-1980s I was becoming aware of the looming dangers and was turning towards the newer movements in philosophy (especially in France) that were anti-Cartesian and anti-individualist. I began to say that the self would have to go. I'd had enough of super-high self-consciousness: as people say, it doesn't get you anywhere. It's disabling and dangerous. I no longer wanted the liberation of the self; I wanted to be liberated from the self, like a Buddhist.

Some of the crucial arguments have already been quoted. Descartes says that I think, therefore I am; I am a thinking thing. Indeed, I am a being whose essence is to think. For Descartes the 'I' is the thinking, self-conscious subject, the real self, a finite spiritual substance, an immortal soul who is in effect a spirit, like an angel. And this being's 'essence' – its defining characteristic – is thinking, which it does all the time.

Descartes wrote at a time when belief in spirits seemed intelligible and even natural, but it doesn't seem so today. I am unable to imagine what a spirit-being could be and I am even less able to conceive what thinking, as its characteristic activity and way of life, could be. I can just about imagine that thinking might be the sort of thing that Hume describes as a stream of tiny mental contents, perceptions, images, ideas and the like, flowing into and then away from the spotlight of our conscious attention. But what Cartesian thinking, as a ghostly counterpart to some bodily activity such as house-building, could be I do not know. Personally, the clearest account I can find of thinking represents it as a disorderly sort of talking to oneself; a scurrying motion of sentences, several at a time and scattering in different directions around the central focus of my attention. This scurrying of sentences is what people may call 'the stream of consciousness' or a 'train of thought'. It is famously pictured as an interior monologue in Molly Bloom's soliloquy at the end of *Ulysses*.[4] But I add the rider that we do more than passively observe a single line of words running by. When our attention is caught, we may fasten upon a word or a phrase, and then we watch associated words and phrases quickly radiating out from it in different directions. Language runs in our heads and we can to some extent track it along branch lines and up dead-ends, like somebody going through a labyrinth until they find the point they are looking for.

When I speak out loud, side tone runs through the bones of my skull to my ears, so that I hear what I am saying as I say it. So easy and habitual is this that we seem to have been able to develop a similar trick in relation to those withheld or unarticulated sentences that are called thoughts. I can, as it were, dimly and inwardly hear the words that are running to the tip of my tongue, but I hold my tongue or bite my tongue and refrain from saying them out loud. And that's all there is to introspective thought. Indeed, it's all there is even to self-consciousness. I am not as grand a being as Descartes, who seems to think that he's an angel in a house of clay; I'm only a talking animal who (sometimes) manages to listen not just to what he says, but to what he's about to say. I pick out and manage to write down a few of the words that every day come rushing unbidden. That, I think, is all that creative thought is; at least it's very much simpler and easier to understand than Descartes' account of thinking as the bodiless activity of a bodiless being.

Now, to complete the demystification of the 'I', we also recall the earlier arguments to the effect that all thought and all our experience is language-wrapped, or linguistically mediated. If that is so and if it is also true, as I have argued, that language – and with it all meanings, all truths and all values – is produced and maintained in the public realm, the space between persons, then the private world of our inner life is in no way primary or founding or privileged. The big 'I' of my subjectivity is nothing special. It is just one secondary privatization of material from the general to-and-fro of cultural life in which we all participate.

What then distinguishes my productions from yours? Why aren't we all very much the same? The answer is that in a society as complex as ours individuals may vary greatly in what they take in each day and what they habitually pay attention to. I have been reading, teaching and writing philosophy and theology very intensively for almost forty years and this must have affected the way language runs spontaneously in my head and the way I pick things out for attention. And that's about it.

From all this I conclude with some relief that there is nothing very special about the first person singular and I sharply disagree with those Jungians and others for whom the 'inner world' is somehow bigger and more real than the outer. Ordinarily the flow of our expressive life should be directed outwards or extravertively. It should flow from us into the public arena and so into the ears of others, and become spread over the public world. This sheds 'brightness'[5] – and some people really do brighten the place up. But sometimes we stop to think and there is a seeming back-projection of 'brightness' that appears to illuminate the inner chamber of the mind. This is only a secondary or reflexive effect, like earthshine on the moon. It is interesting, but not so very important and some excellent people hardly ever pay it any attention at all.

I am wary of Kierkegaard now. Certainly I no longer equate religiousness with preoccupation with one's own inwardness or subjectivity. On the contrary, I'm inclined rather to admire those people who never give their souls a thought because they are so completely absorbed in serving their fellow humans or in love of the world or in artistic expression. I'd like to be so extraverted

that I have no self at all. We are taught the 'I' – perhaps by way
of instilling into us ideas of personal identity and continuing
moral and legal responsibility – but otherwise we might be so
given over to objectivity that we never get round to identifying
the 'I' at all. I'd like that.

13

Our world

So far as we are concerned it was Wittgenstein who said it first and said it most clearly: the primary world is the world that is given to each and every one of us by and within ordinary language. A world is a sort of stage or setting for our life. It provides us with a 'scene' or milieu in which we can act, express ourselves and generally do our thing and it also functions as a market-place in which we can enter into a variety of exchange-relationships with each other. Evidently I'm describing a human world, our world, a world that has become fully appropriated by human beings and which in every sense supports human life. Such a fully humanized world has at last come into being only quite recently, with the coming of the liberal democratic state, the industrial revolution and the very rapid growth of modern science and technology. For us the world has now become our world to such an extent that it is now hard to imagine and hard to remember how very different things formerly were.

In the earliest times the world in no sense belonged to human beings. There was almost no theory and no understanding of the causes of things. Human beings saw themselves as the mere spectators of great conflicts between uncomprehended cosmic powers and forces that were quite indifferent to the puny humans who observed – and sometimes found themselves caught up in the violence of – their battles. In Iron Age times, when ideas of a relatively stable and unified cosmic order had developed, humans would often dub it fate, necessity or destiny and would still see themselves as being simply its victims. Even ethical theism was usually predestinarian, and as late as Luther that very great figure could still speak of the human being as a mere beast who must be ridden, either by God or by the Devil. Only very gradually and over a very long period have human beings succeeded in fully appropriating their own world. Think: belief in ghosts, in spirits and in monsters was still quite vivid even within living memory.

However, there has also been since early times a belief that the world was originally designed to be our world and that the first human beings did actually live in an earthly paradise, a garden-world expressly made for them and given to them. In Eden there are no spirits or monsters and the serpent is only a serpent. All the beasts have been named by the man, which implies appropriation. God, too, looks like and walks about like a man. So the world at least began by being fully our world and the long epic narrative of Fall and Redemption promises the reappropriation of the world to humankind at the end of history – Paradise regained through the work of the second Adam. And indeed the classic Majestas image of Christ in early and eastern Christian art pictures him as enthroned over the cosmos, the man who rules all the world.

I argue, then, that a very large part of the spiritual history of humanity has been taken up with a great struggle to make *the* world into *our* world. In the German tradition and in Marxism we hear talk of 'world-mastery' and of 'the conquest of nature', but we should avoid that language. It invites obvious retorts about the unpredictability and the destructiveness of earthquakes and storms. Instead, we should speak of the way we have thoroughly familiarized the world to ourselves by describing and theorizing every bit of it. Our language has become interwoven with the world so ubiquitously and so profoundly that apart from and prior to our language, all that now remains is simply the airy featherlight forthcomingness of be-ing. We have familiarized the world to ourselves and made it our world to such a degree that we can be quite confident that no rival or enemy is in the least likely to come forward and dispute our possession of it. We have thus effectively completed the historical project; we have made *the* world into *our* world. And in so doing, we have also completed the project of religion, at least in the form we have known it hitherto. Hierarchy-led, disciplinary, marching-through-the-wilderness-type religion has recently completely its task,[1] and is now due not merely for another *ecdysis* (a shiny new version of the same outer form) but for metamorphosis into its imago, its final and adult stage of life, when it at last becomes winged and sexually mature (because, as you will have gathered, this is an insect metaphor).[2]

Now if this isn't startling enough, our eyes open wider still when we recognize the extent to which ordinary language has already got there. Systemically, and for 'structural' reasons, the world-view that is built into ordinary language anticipates – not expects, but tries to seize and enjoy prematurely – the end of history.[3]

Consider this: language evolved simply as the human communication-system. It is therefore scarcely surprising that it pictures the world as being – proximately at least – a human communications-network. Human beings are such compulsive communicators that Israelis, who in the 1970s when I lived amongst them for a while seemed never to stop talking, today manage to be the world's leading users of mobile phones as well. We are such compulsive communicators that when your daughter gets home from school she needs to make straight for the telephone in order to catch up on what her best friends have been doing since they parted from each other outside the school gates fifteen minutes ago. It is scarcely surprising that in so many idioms your 'world' is simply your circle of friends.

Almost our whole tradition attaches a uniquely high value to the intimate fellowship and the networking of a society of fully reconciled persons. The messianic age, the kingdom of God, heaven and the new Jerusalem are described in these terms throughout the religious tradition, from the Israelite prophets through to modern socialism, both religious and secular. The same theme is prominent in German philosophy from Hegel to Habermas. And without anyone very much remarking upon the fact, ordinary language has also postulated and taught us to strive for just such a state of affairs. It had to.

Ordinary language, however, does not quite go all the way

with radical humanism. It pictures us as being still surrounded and threatened by an impersonal 'it' or 'it all' that eludes our full understanding and control. We must try to set it aside or keep it at bay, if we are to keep all our lines of communication with each other fully open. This 'it', *das Es*, is rather like what Freud locates in our psychology and calls the Id and is also close to what the later Lacan calls 'the real' – 'that which resists symbolization', something obstinate and elusive that we cannot familiarize to ourselves by taking it into our language. At any rate, ordinary language pictures us as being close to the fully humanized world that we have always desired, but not quite there yet. We are still troubled by the residues of old terrors not yet completely banished.

Meanwhile, we observe that what our religious tradition has always hoped for, what our politics of liberation has always hoped for and what ordinary language must posit and strive for, are one and the same!

The question now arises of how our language can be the cosmic logos that penetrates everywhere, forming everything and familiarizing it to us. How does language tame everything and calm things down?

My first suggestion starts from the way animals use sign-language and symbolic displays in order to make competition between males, courtship, competition for a place on the breeding-grounds and other stressful activities less tense and dangerous.[4] As Churchill once remarked, jaw-jaw is better than war-war; provided that the initial dispute does indeed get settled, a symbolic conflict without anyone getting injured is much to be preferred to a real conflict. But any symbolic expression has to be general in order to be intelligible and both the sender and the receiver must recognize and abide by the rules of the game; and so it is that by turning the rut (for example) into a well-understood language-game that stags make their lives more predictable and peaceful. Both for deer and for early human beings the way of things in the life-world looks at first to be terrifyingly violent and uncertain, especially while it remains undescribed and 'nameless', but language used within the setting of generally recognized language-games has huge power to structure the course of life and make things more intelligible, more predictable and more peaceful. And science does just that job: the process of the world seemed to our early ancestors extremely capricious, but science ritualizes or routinizes the process of the world, by describing things and by bringing them under rule and so making it very much easier for us to tell what to expect next. Science familiarizes the world to us by describing it in very carefully used standard terminology and by routinizing it, bringing it under rule in very much the same way as animals use a long sequence of symbolic behaviours and rituals to get themselves successfully and unhurt through the rigours of the annual breeding season.

Second, not only does language mitigate the violence of the world by bringing it under standard descriptions and rules and not only do standard symbolic behaviours exercise a moderating influence upon the relations between individuals, language can also reconcile conflicting forces within individuals and help them to get themselves together.

To see how this happens we begin with the Freudian doctrine that the neurotic symptom is a 'compromise-formation'. It is a sign, almost a piece of language, that both reveals and conceals the powerful impulse that drives it – the typical case being that of an urgent but forbidden wish that insists on finding some kind of expression, but which cannot be expressed directly. So it appears in disguise, as the symptom. To interpret the symptom we must deconstruct it, reading it in such a way as to reveal the play of forces that has shaped it.

Now we may develop this idea into a doctrine about linguistic expression generally. We picture the human being as a system of forces that struggle to come out into expression. We are trying to 'get ourselves together' by 'coming out', but this is not easy because the forces of which we are composed are in many ways at odds with each other. So we seek forms of symbolic expression through which we can become relatively unified expressed selves. We do this in our behaviours, our utterances and our products, all of which may on deconstructive analysis show themselves to be the results of a play of forces. There is always a subtext, always a little gap between what you are ostensibly saying and what you are really getting at. (Your partner invariably hears the latter.)

It follows from this that the self is not an immortal spiritual substance but only a process of symbolic expression in time. Like a fountain, it is pouring out and passing away continually. Or it is a story that is being told only once. 'That's the story of my life,' people say. The self is essentially fleeting or transient, an effect of language. It is made of language, which is why psychoanalysis from the very first was evidently something very like literary criticism. Freud was interpreting the stream of signs given off by his patient.

In our present quoting of these ideas, note that we are not following in the Schopenhauer/Freud tradition that regards the instinctual drives or the will or whatever as the noumenal reality that underlies the world in general and our life in particular. The forces disclosed need not be more than interpretative devices, things we postulate when we are trying to account for people's behaviour. What we do stick with is the view – I think the correct view – that the self exists only within its own transient symbolic expression. There is no 'real me'; there is only the *dramatis persona*, the role being played.

14

Reality and the imagination

What is 'objective reality'? Objective means literally thrown-out, over-there, and something is said to be objectively real if it exists quite independently of us – which means usually, independent of our minds: independent, that is, of our sense-experience of it, our consciousness of it, our knowledge of it and our particular way of describing and theorizing it.

A difficulty is immediately obvious: how can I verify realism? How can I check that things exist independently of my mind or consciousness? As soon as I apply the test to make sure that something is really out there, independent of my thought of it, I am bringing it to my mind. I am in the silly position of a beginner in philosophy, worrying about George Berkeley's ideas, who turns his head very quickly to check if the tree's still there when he's not looking at it. Sorry; you can't verify realism that way. You need either a philosophical argument or independent confirmation.

In the older pre-Enlightenment world – and even today, perhaps, in the Muslim world – some people reckon that they can make short work of this problem of establishing objective reality by starting from God. The supreme and unchallengeable case of real and objective existence is God, who has revealed himself. He has declared his own reality. He has made himself known to us. And God, being revealed, confers a derived objectivity on all the things with which he concerns himself: the created world, truth, the human soul and the moral order.

In theistic cultures there is thus an overwhelmingly great independent guarantor of objective reality, namely God. Believing in God, most Jews, Christians and Muslims have tended to assume theological realism and all that goes with it. It still seems obvious to most believers that we have been planted in a ready-made and fully furnished cosmos, with an intelligible order built in and a moral order already in place. What is more, we have been created with the intellectual capacities needed to help us to know the cosmic order and understand the moral law.

This is fine; and many or most people are no doubt still realists in that old pre-Enlightenment sense. In recent years there have also been a few Christian theologians and many Muslims who have attempted to conquer what they see as post-modern 'nihilism' by theological positivism – loudly asserting the objective reality of a God who has declared himself and who also effectively guarantees the created order that he has established. But in the history of philosophy George Berkeley was the last notable figure to invoke God to guarantee objectivity.[1] The main thrust of Enlightenment thought was to try to rebuild the world around the human subject and to try to find a purely human justification for the objectivity of human knowledge, without invoking God. This means that after Hume and Kant the question of realism was bound to become very prominent. Without the help of the old independent guarantor, how could you jump unaided across the wide gap between human subjective experience and extra-human objective reality? How can you get real objectivity out of mere subjectivity? All our knowledge of the world depends upon jiggles and twitches in our sensory nerves, and how can such jiggles and twitches ever assure us of the existence of anything beyond themselves?

Nobody has found the problem easy, for the past 250 years. Hume was a conservative sort of sceptic, who fell back upon our 'natural belief' in objective reality. Thomas Reid (1710–96), like G. E. Moore more recently, was a 'natural realist', who appealed to 'commonsense'. Kant sought both to show how we do, and to prove that we must, confer objectivity upon the known world as we build it; so he founded the tradition of German Idealism. In more recent times a new type of solution as been found, as many philosophers have tried to escape from the old obsessive concern for objective reality and the objectivity of our knowledge; they are the non-realists, such as the pragmatists and the followers of Wittgenstein. They ask us to forget metaphysics and urge us to be content to let our knowledge be simply what it is; we should not fret about our inability to prove that it passes an impossible (and unnecessary) test. Human knowledge does not need to be purely objective or absolute knowledge in the old sense. It is enough for our knowledge to be human, as we are. We do not need to dream of having godlike knowledge.[2]

Today it is sometimes said that the dispute between realists and non-realists is no longer a live issue. Many theologians (being professionally accustomed to clutching at straws) are taking it that non-realism is therefore no longer a 'threat' and that they can go back to theological realism. They radically misunderstand the situation. The true position is that we no longer wish to convert *our* world back into *the* world. We no longer want to try to give to our human knowledge a kind of metaphysical guarantee of objectivity that would mean nothing to it and that is not going to be forthcoming anyway. In short, we no longer feel the old realist impulse and non-realism no longer frightens us. *Our* world is fine, just as such. We are non-realists who have forgotten realism and therefore no longer need to bother with the word non-realism either.

Ethics is a case in point. Nietzsche thought that the end of moral realism was a catastrophic event. But we, with our talk of human values, human rights and our admirable humanitarian ethics, accept ethical non-realism and take its truth for granted, without turning a hair. Of course we invented morality. It's human, and no less precious to us for that. Morality has to be human and we no longer need to suppose that it is anything else.

In 1946, Sartre gave a lecture titled 'Existentialism is a humanism' – meaning, in effect, there's no need to be frightened of existentialism. Today we could similarly give a lecture called 'Nihilism is a humanism': with the world comprehensively appropriated to ourselves, all the old objectively real things-out-there gone and no 'substances' left, we find that radical humanism coincides with nihilism – and it is easy and friendly. Who's afraid of the big bad wolf of nihilism?

Very well, you may say, but why are realistic tendencies, like original sin or bourgeois impulses, so ubiquitous? We need an error theory to explain people's inveterate desire for a kind of reality that is not available to us and wouldn't do us any good even if we had it. Here's the answer: we tend to fall into realism for reasons of laziness, efficiency, consensus, exculpation and power.

Laziness

Like other creatures, we tend to drop into habits of thought and action. It saves effort and it's very comfortable to be able to follow familiar routines unthinkingly. Soon, one's world-view and habits become set in concrete; they become a reality that it seems impossible to change. Familiar metaphors speak of a stick-in-the-mud, who is bogged down and in a rut, bound by the chains of habit. Such a person's world has become for him/her *the* world, and he/she cannot and will not change it. He/she has become a sort of realist.

Efficiency

Since the very beginnings of the first industrial revolution in the early modern period, western culture has become gradually more dominated by the search for greater efficiency – for example, in the organization of production and in the management of time and resources. Our life has become very highly routinized and natural science has obliged by constructing an equally highly routinized vision of the physical world and even of the biological world. Efficiency makes for survival. But this domination of world-view and life by considerations of engineering efficiency itself tends to create a formidable reality that becomes very difficult to challenge. Notoriously, even people who are aware that the scientific picture of the world changes very rapidly are still strongly inclined to dogmatic realism about present scientific theory.

Consensus

As has been mentioned earlier, the consent of the faithful was invoked in Christendom as a criterion of truth.[3] During the sixteenth and seventeenth centuries the idea began to migrate, first to the Republic of Letters and then to the scientific societies and academies, where it proved a huge success. Today, everyone knows that if you want your knowledge-system to enjoy high social esteem, you must impose a strict 'regime of truth' (a phrase from Foucault) upon your profession. A well-policed consensus creates a very strong effect of reality and truth.

Exculpation

People appeal to 'reality' and to 'the real world' by way of pooh-poohing youthful idealism and justifying their own sharp practice. 'Get real!' they say, 'everybody's doing it', and they suggest that we have no option but to follow the local mores. Here, the motive for invoking a 'reality' that may be declared but cannot be altered is the need to exculpate oneself. The non-realist is a person who thinks that the world and 'human nature' can be changed, but the realist is a pessimist who says that they cannot. An extreme and amusing case of Christian realism is the sort of wealthy right-wing protestant who so presses the themes of original sin and the wickedness of the world that for him/her Christianity is a faith that in this life we need only believe. In the world as it is, the Sermon on the Mount is not practicable. So we cannot reasonably be expected actually to practise our religion until the kingdom comes or after death. The late J. Enoch Powell MP took the view of this type.

Power

The one who has the greatest power, the one whose word is law, is the one who creates the reality of the situation, the framework within which we must live and act. This principle is most familiar to us in religion, but it has very wide application in human affairs.

Enough now has been said to show that, as well as the old metaphysical realism, usually founded in Plato's metaphysics or in God, there is also still current a wide range of idioms about the moral and social realities within which we live. This sort of reality is rather variously generated and is thought severely to restrict our freedom of action. People invoke it by way of explaining that we cannot expect to be able to change ourselves or human nature in general or the world. Realists have a very strong sense of the weight of the powers that be.

Against this background we may well wonder how it comes about that so many people assign the moral high ground to realism and regard anti-realism or nihilism as being shocking and wicked. The truth of the matter is the other way round. Humanistic and 'active' nihilism of the sort that I have described reacts sharply against the moral cynicism and pessimism of the realists. It asserts our complete appropriation of our world to ourselves and therefore our entire responsibility for our world. It stresses art, human creativity and the power of the utopian imagination. Why shouldn't we reimagine and remake our world and ourselves? The real world of the realists is an iron cage created by their own sloth, moral cowardice and fascination with power. The humanistic nihilist wants to liberate people to remake this sorry scheme of things entire. So it is not obvious that nihilism commands the moral high ground? Of course it does.

A very old tradition in philosophy, going back to the pre-socratics, seeks to produce an effect of illumination by saying that everything is so-and-so. The account I have been giving revolves around three gestures of that type. Let us call them the truth of poetry, the truth of Buddhism and the truth of Idealism.

The truth of poetry declares that 'all is language', the flux of signs. Language embraces everything. In the beginning was the word and in the dance of language everything, including ourselves, is produced and held. Language lures forth being and language generates consciousness.

The truth of Buddhism declares that 'all is fleeting, transient being', the fountain, the pitter-patter of quantum fluctuations in the vacuum. Everything quietly, gently, continuously pours out into objective symbolic expression and then passes away.

The truth of Idealism declares that 'all is brightness, consciousness, knowledge'. We humans – we don't know why – are the place where everything becomes conscious of itself and brightly lit. That aesthetic–religious joy, of which every human being has known something, is what makes it all worthwhile.

Now, if our philosophical situation is as I have described it, how is the individual to live? What sort of religious outlook and practice is appropriate for him/her? That question is to be dealt with in the third part of this book.

Part Three: The Teaching

15

Dissemination

Half a century after the impact of Wittgenstein and Heidegger, our philosophical situation is as I have described it. Not everyone will agree with me, for there are plenty of Enlightenment conservatives around and plenty of irrationalists and special pleaders of one kind and another. Nor can I venture the claim that most people will one day agree with me. No, alas, for it may well be that our future is to be merely 'technology, entertainment, fundamentalism' (and therewith, war). What I have outlined is a kind of best-case scenario. This is how one hopes it will be. This is how things now are for the people who care most about philosophy, and if there continue to be such people this is (I think) how they will generally see things in fifty or a hundred years' time.

It is an optimistic vision. It allows one to hope that in the future people will believe that we can remake ourselves and remake our world, that we can love life in its very contingency and transience and that we can find intense religious–aesthetic joy in everything's 'brightness' (which is to be explained further).

I do, then, envisage a future for religion, but not much of a future for religion as we have known it hitherto. So far, for the majority of the human race, religion has involved dealings with a 'higher' or supernatural Being or order of beings or world. The higher Being or beings are seen as having created us and as having given us the moral law. How they feel about us is of the utmost importance to us. We desperately need their favour. Fortunately for us, they have intervened in human affairs in order to reveal their disposition towards us and tell us how we can win their favour. And so on: historically, most of religion –

especially in the West – has involved substantial bodies of super-natural belief. Since we obviously do not have any direct access to the supernatural world, it is usually said that religious faith is dogmatic belief held upon authority – whether the authority of the Bible alone or of the scriptures as they are interpreted within and by the religious community.

Today, in spite of the great popularity of Buddhism in the modern West, most of us still strongly associate religion with supernatural belief. Such people will surely conclude that if our philosophical situation is as I have described it, religion can have no future at all. For in the philosophical outlook I have pre-sented, there is no supernatural order whatever. It does not figure. There are no 'mysteries' either, if by mysteries one means loopholes for irrationalism. There is only Be-ing (which is not any thing, but only the pure contingent forthcomingness and transience of everything) and the motion of language, and the production of language-formed human selfhood in a language-formed world. The only additional item is the 'brightness' or lit-upness of everything. Such is my analysis of what is por-tentously called 'ultimate reality'; that is all there is, and it leaves no room for traditional supernaturalist religion and therefore no room for dogmatic faith. If we already live in the last world and it is wholly our world, there is no room or need for beliefs about any beyond. There is certainly room for ethical striving to better ourselves and our world, but not for any sort of supernatural belief.

Are there, however, any good reasons why we may still see some wisdom in humankind's religious traditions and may perhaps attempt to demythologize and modernize them? Given their moral and intellectual record, are we justified in trying to prolong the lives of one or more of our received religions?

I'd say a cautious yes, for three reasons. First, Buddhism's core intellectual tradition, only now becoming better known in the West, is very high-quality and it is non-supernaturalist.[1] It is a mine that is by no means yet exhausted. Second, there is a notable strand of religious humanism in the Jewish/Christian tradition, which has become more explicit and prominent since the Enlightenment, and third, Christianity has a vital strand in it that actually looks forward to its own self-transcendence at the end of historical time, as the church gives way to the kingdom. It turns out that the world-view of Kingdom-Christianity is very close to the radical-humanist philosophy that I have described.[2]

However, the philosophy of religion, as I use the phrase in this book, is not an historical subject and it is not apologetics on behalf of any particular historical religion. We are simply asking how current philosophy sees the human condition and what religious possibilities it opens up for us. And the argument so far has suggested that there are five things that religion today might be.

1 Religion might be meditative attention to Be-ing, the purely contingent forthcomingness of everything.

2 Religion might be seen as involving attention to language and in particular the world of religious signs and symbols, many of which remain current in everyday speech despite the seeming scepticism of the times.

3 Religion might be seen as involving an attempt to re-imagine and remake the self.

4 Religion might be seen as involving an attempt to re-imagine and remake our world – which means, in particular, the social world.

5 Religion might be joy in the 'brightness' of the whole world of temporal Being, as it becomes fully developed by language. To me, at least, this brightness is a sort of world-joy, gratuitous, mysterious and wonderful.

In setting out to deal with this syllabus, we first remark on another reason why we cannot simply continue or revise one of the major traditions that has come down to us historically. It is that in post-modernity the cultural world has become very scattered and multi-faith. The old structuring of the whole of life by a single great tradition has broken down, as the old religious control of language and iconography has broken down. The result is that fragments of religious language and terminology are

now disseminated very widely across the culture. The outcome –
religion minus its old structure, religion minus metaphysics,
ubiquitous in scattered appearances with no underlying reality –
resembles the philosophical doctrine that used to be called
phenomenalism. But let me explain.

A curious feature of many large religious symbol-systems is that
they are governed by two conflicting organizing principles: one
demanding universality and the other seeking hierarchical
organization and concentration. The former principle declares
that whatever is true in religion is true everywhere, for everyone,
all the time, but the latter principle structures space, time and
society in such a way as to concentrate each particular doctrinal
theme at one season of the year, in one site and even perhaps in
one person, more than elsewhere.

Thus God is everywhere – but somehow is pictured architecturally as being concentrated just beyond and above the east end
of the church interior. God is equidistant from each of us and not
far from any of us – but we may nevertheless be enjoined to
'draw near' to God. Christ is always one who has already 'come'
amongst us – but he comes a bit more at Advent, and more
still at Christmas. In addition, there are prayers for a further
eschatological coming still awaited: *Maranatha*.

Thus the principle that religious truth is universal co-exists
with another principle that works to structure space, time and
the religious society and makes some times, places and persons
appear to be very much more sacred than others. The working-
out of the latter principle makes the world rather complicated,
because the machinery that operates to concentrate the sacred in
one site not only leaves a large area of life common, ordinary or
secular, but in many cases also creates a forbidden unclean zone,
to which is consigned everything that was forcibly excluded in
order to create the extra-sacred image.

A familiar example of this is the Christian symbol of the
Blessed Virgin Mary with her child, the infant Christ. Mary's
appearance is rather nun-like. Only her hands and her face are
exposed and her breast appears only at feeding-time. Her

husband is an older, shadowy figure in the background; she never looks at him. She is not a wife, but only and wholly a mother. The iconography, like standard doctrine, emphasizes how different she is from any other woman, so that the image of the Madonna and Child implicitly secularizes the experience of ordinary women. More than that, doctrine and iconography very firmly exclude any thought of her female sexuality and her female reproductive apparatus – so firmly as to make them into something forbidden and unclean. Thus in Catholic Christian art, the male genitalia are quite often exposed in works installed in churches, but the female – never. The image of a woman looking very pleased about her male child is one of the commonest and most popular of all art-subjects. Corresponding images of a woman looking equally pleased about her female child do exist: they portray St Anne, with her child Mary. But they are very, very uncommon and they give one a shock. Ask yourself: how can the Christian artist make evident the fact that Anne's baby is a girl? We never developed the vocabulary to say such a thing.

After all this, it is not surprising that images of those aspects of her that are repressed return like a swarm of noxious insects in Chris Ofili's notorious recent painting, *The Holy Virgin Mary*; and it is also not surprising that feminists are so critical of the way woman is represented in Christian art and thought. Just one thing can be pointed out in reply to them: it is that the popular tradition, exemplified by for example the many black Virgins, is much better and more varied than the official theology.

In general, I am suggesting that the religious structuring of time in the canonical hours and the liturgical year, of space into many different forms and degrees of sacred and profane space and of persons in many degrees of personal holiness and sacred rank – all this organizes culture and makes the world more manageable and interesting. But, as we have said, any great concentration of the sacred at one point in space or time tends to create a drained profane zone around it and in many cases also creates a dangerous forbidden and unclean region from which in future trouble may come. (There is a good indication of the character of this underworld region in the iconography of Hell in the various religions. One should look at the way demons are portrayed and at the nature of the torments they inflict. Hell equals what has been and must remain repressed.) Furthermore, we must note that wherever there is a great concentration of the sacred there is likely also to be found a high priest who wields considerable spiritual power, for good and ill. In the past, abuse of spiritual power has been so common that it is not surprising that there has recently been such a very sharp reaction against it and indeed against the whole religious structuring of the life-world.

During the twentieth century the long-established distinction between the sacred and the profane was erased by the general triumph of the profane and the collapse and levelling of the old religious structuring of life. Most of the remaining strongholds of the sacred were absorbed by the heritage industry and converted into tourist attractions. People simply lost their sense of the holy. The power of the religious authorities to police religious language and to protect religious symbolism against profanation failed and, as a result, religious themes, emotions and symbols floated free of their old moorings and became scattered across the whole of the life-world, with consequences that vary from kitsch religiosity to high seriousness. The death of God – that is, the end of metaphysics – has resulted in a general immanentiza-tion of the divine that many people find disorienting and para-doxical.[3]

On the one hand, it seems that none of us is a straightforward 'orthodox' believer any longer. Supernatural belief and religious authority have weakened too much. The 'devoutly religious' are not clearly visible as a distinct group within the population, identifiable by their behaviour and vocabulary, at all.

Yet, on the other hand, the diffusion of religious language and symbolism across the whole face of experience means that in many ways we are now far more religious than ever before. In the old world most of life was backbreaking labour with much hardship and sickness, all relieved only by a few hours on Sunday enjoying a magically beautiful foretaste of a better world here-after. But in our new world almost all of our experience has a religious flavour. Every day we enjoy moments of exaltation, of sympathy, of joy, of visual rapture and of at-one-ness such as once were the privilege of mystics. The very degree of consciousness that we almost all of us now enjoy was only a few centuries ago still restricted to a tiny handful of the very gifted.

In our post-modernity almost all of our experience is religious, at least in the sense of being coloured or flavoured by language derived from religion, and very often also in the stronger sense of being itself redeployed religious experience. I have elsewhere attempted to demonstrate this point from the new idioms that have been coming and are still coming into our everyday speech, but the same job could be done in other ways, for example by showing how the new helping professions continue the pastoral work and a good deal of the language and the outlook, of the clergy in former days.

Still more important, though, is the point that we are amongst the first people who do not believe either in life after death or in progress and therefore our experience is remarkably free of ulteriority. We are amongst the first people who are not living this life in preparation for or in expectation of any kind of better life hereafter. We are already living at the end of the world – that is, in a world that no longer has any further world beyond it. This is your life, this is your one and only life, so you must make the most of it and live it to the full. Accordingly, ordinary people now commit themselves to life, just this life, more wholeheartedly than anybody has done since Nietzsche's 'only Christian' delivered the Sermon on the Mount.[4] The death of God has made the common people Christian at last!

In Christianity religious instruction usually takes the form of doctrinal teaching by expounding the scriptures. By contrast, the typical practice in Buddhism is for a well-known monk to 'give a teaching', often without notes. It consists simply of informal religious instruction. In this book the account of religion that I am giving does not appeal to any scriptures and is non-doctrinal. Hence the title of this part: The Teaching. It will be summarized in a sentence or two at the end of each chapter, thus:

The whole of life is religious. With the erasure of the distinction between the sacred and the profane, religious meaning and value have been scattered, somewhat irregularly, across the whole life-world.

16

Easy, going

Until the early nineteenth century the western tradition in philosophy and religion was broadly agreed in ascribing the highest value and general importance to whatever was eternal rather than merely temporal, necessary rather than merely contingent, infinite rather than finite and changeless and incorruptible rather than changeable and corruptible. The five binary contrasts cited were sealed into western thought by Plato along with a number of others (for example, universal/particular, noumenal/phenomenal, reason/the passions, and long-term blessedness versus short-term gratification), the effect of them all together being to create a broad contrast between two worlds or orders of reality – one close at hand, which we live in, and the other, higher and greater, which we should look to and steer by. Human life was seen as a pilgrimage through time towards the eternal world. In order to keep on the right course we should never allow ourselves to be guided by the needs of the body or by short-term desires and impulses, but should always think long term and look up to the eternal world, like a sea-captain who navigates by the stars.

Plato, like the Buddha, lived in an age of political instability and warring city states, a time when thoughtful people could scarcely fail to regard the violence of the passions as a serious threat to long-term human well-being. One of the most important tasks of the philosopher, as of the teacher of wisdom before him, was to supply rulers with self-disciplined and cool-headed counsellors who could calm down the hotheads by appealing to the big picture and the long-term interests of the state. In that context, the criticism of the passions by Plato and the Buddha makes a lot of sense. But when their teaching is applied to the individual's personal ethic and lifestyle, serious doubts arise.

There are three main points of difficulty. The first is that in platonism 'the soul' is always in some degree at odds with 'the body'. The body is animal, it knows only its own desires and passions and it is headed only for death. The body is purely of this world below, whereas the soul is almost a spirit. It is naturally immortal and rational and is in exile while it remains here below. It longs to return to its true home in the world above. The body? – a leaden jacket, holding the soul down. But in retrospect this picture of the human being as inwardly divided and suspended between two very different worlds seems very odd indeed. Why sentence yourself to lifelong unhappiness and mistrust of your own body? But it is how people used to think: in England lyric poets were still writing dialogues between the soul and the body that emphasized the dispute between them until the late seventeenth century. And it is worth adding that the religious devalorization of the body and its claims has in the past been particularly hard upon women.

The second difficulty arises over ulteriorism. In platonism, and in the Roman Catholic moral theology that prevailed until very recently, you were taught to be extremely long-termist. Reason was equated with due regard for long-term considerations to such an extent that your every act had to be assessed in terms of its bearing upon your own eternal salvation. There seemed to be no way of giving their due moral weight to the claims of the body, the senses, the passions, this life and the present moment. Plato's scheme of values puts abstract philosophical thought above all else and cannot cope at all, for example, with the sensuousness and the particularity of art.

The third difficulty is that the whole scheme of thought is only as good as the belief in life after death. Plato's own arguments on this topic in the *Phaedo* are very feeble[1] and nobody else since his day has done any better. Although in general people are extraordinarily tenacious in holding on to their traditional beliefs, since Darwin it has become about as clear as can be that this one must at last be given up. In which case religious long-termism is mistaken, for as Keynes said, in the long run we're all dead.[2]

The last great philosophical system to be constructed still within Plato's framework was that of Kant. After him, a conscious 'revaluation of values' begins to take place amongst the Romantics and within the developing tradition of German idealism. As people begin to see all of reality as developing process, Plato's timeless noumenal world is evacuated. Reason, thought and world-view are brought down into history and are seen themselves to have histories. The old timeless forms become ideas with writable histories. Even the passions have histories. The Romantics themselves had not merely revalued the passions; they'd invented some new and wildly popular ones.

These vast cultural changes have been assimilated in an irregular way over a very long period. Curiously, the painters were quickest off the mark in switching attention to the things of this world. In Italy the background colour of religious paintings was already changing from gold to blue, from Heaven to this world, as early as Giotto. Soon after the Reformation in northern Europe, painting becomes a celebration of ordinary people and domestic life. And, in all this, painting was far ahead of philosophy.

It was also well ahead of religion. To a surprising degree standard Christian doctrine, both Latin and Greek, remains a picturesque comic-book version of platonism to this day. The same is true of standard Christian spirituality; the values implicit in the monk's way of life still owe much more to Plato than to Christ.

Eventually, however, the end of platonism and the gradual emergence of a thoroughly and consistently post-platonic and this-worldly outlook is sure to cause a revolution in religious values. The most obvious has to do with the question of Being. After Parmenides and Plato, western religion developed as the solitary contemplation and the public worship of God as eternal, self-existent and perfect Being. But after Kant, Schelling and Hegel begin to see Being itself as temporally unfolding process. Today, the only form in which we can rightly practise traditional contemplation is by attention to the forthcoming of Be-ing, a present participle that signifies a gentle, continuous outflow-in-time of pure contingency. I suggest that the best way to do this is by watching, in a state of relaxed attention, a simple natural motion like the movement of a cloud. (Take ten minutes.) Be-ing itself is not any thing. It is even less of an object than God; it is prior to all experience and prior to language and should perhaps be written Heidegger-fashion as B̶e̶ing. But because the forth-coming of Be-ing and the passing of time are so intimately bound up together, watching a gentle natural motion like that of the sea or of a cloud is the nearest one can get to contemplating Be-ing.

The cloud is easy, going – and so should we be. We have abandoned Plato's contrast between real, eternal Being and mere temporal Becoming, and instead have brought Being and time together in the simple word Be-ing. We now understand all reality as flowing, temporal and continuously renewed. But this calls for thoroughgoing religious acceptance of universal con-tingency – and especially, of our own contingency. Everything is hap; that is, it just happens to be. Nothing either compels it to be so or guarantees that it will remain so. So can we get used to, can we become really easy and relaxed about our own contingency and transience? It is not easy, but it can be done. We need first to give up the idea of the self as a substance and then we need to give up the old western idea that our first task is to secure our own salvation. We do better to join the Mahayana Buddhist, who actually takes a vow to put his own salvation not first of all, but last of all. I readily acknowledge that one can be made to pay heavily for not having had a sufficient regard for one's own personal happiness. The self does have a claim. But in the West there has been too much religious self-examination and too much interest in the drama of one's own 'inner life'. On the whole it is better to be outward-looking and to put the world and one's work ahead of oneself. On the whole it is better to be light rather than serious about 'existence', a point Kierkegaard once made with reference to Luke 17.10 by saying that we should strive with all our might in the knowledge that all our striving is but a jest. As the beautiful English idiom goes, make light of it.

Some people find the lightness unbearable, because somehow they cannot bear the thought that our knowledge, our values and our various forms of life have no assured permanence and no objective underwriting at all. The only consolation I offer is to point to the outsidelessness of our world. All this of ours is all there is, so do not be troubled by the thought of a vast emptiness out there that mocks us. There is no mockery. There is no outside viewpoint. There's only all this of ours and it is enough for us. Your values are as good as your own loyalty to them and if nothing supports you by guaranteeing them, neither is anything going to rob you of them. It's all yours.

A second consolatory argument points out that we are now in the position that God was in, according to the traditional theology, before he created the world. God is infinite, perfect and pure act. He has no unfulfilled potential and no wants. In fact he can have no motives at all. So why should God create the worlds of angels and men, particularly when he foreknows what a lot of hassle it is all going to cause him? The best answer given was that God creates out of an overflow of creative energy and love, out of his will to expression and self-giving. He desires that there should be a theatre in which his glory is revealed. He wants to see himself reflected in a sort of Other. Applied to ourselves, this line of talk suggests that we must posit and pursue our values, love life and do our work, all just for the joy of it and completely disinterestedly. We must be good for nothing or even (as people sometimes say) good just for the Hell of it – meaning, I suppose, that one feels confident enough to be able to act gratuitously, and refuses even to think about explaining or justifying oneself.

A more spectacular test is Nietzsche's. He speaks of getting himself in the right mood to do philosophy by picturing himself as the very last man. He is dying alone in a vast desert; vultures circle above him. When his consciousness finally blacks out, the whole universe will lapse into endless night. It will be all over. So with what is he to occupy himself during his remaining minutes, before all thought becomes extinct?

I do not recommend anyone else to hype him/herself up to do philosophy in such an intense and strenuous way as Nietzsche did. It is highly inadvisable. But if we can imagine using his test, we may understand his answer: one should simply say Yes to life and express oneself in the present moment and disdain to look for any sort of backing or encouragement or payback. Hence Nietzsche's admiration for the aristocrat's self-confidence and his mistrust of self-consciousness. We should just go ahead and do our thing, without worrying about getting permission or justification or applause or forgiveness or an excuse. Just do it! Interestingly, when a student said to Wittgenstein, 'What's the point of doing anything, when in a hundred years we'll all be dead, and it won't make any difference?' he reacted sharply and along the same lines. He simply refused to take that sort of worry seriously.

Why? And in particular, why did Wittgenstein so disdain popular philosophy's doubts about 'the meaning of life' that he scarcely bothered to reply to them? Perhaps he thought that the doubts were like those of a child who is shown a globe of the Earth. 'And this is England', the child is told, as a finger prods the globe near the top. The child wonders about the tropics. Don't people there find it difficult to hold on? And what about Australia – how does it feel to be walking about upside-down? Now the adult needs to explain how it is that wherever you are is the top. We can see that we are on top of the world, by the way things go down over the horizon all around us. And that's how it also is for other people all around the world, including the Australians. We never come to the edge of the world and we never really feel that we are down under. For all of us, wherever we are is the top of the world. So there is no reason why the fact that they seem on the globe to be upside down relative to us should cause Australians any anxiety at all. And in the same way we never step outside life, nor come to any region where our values are somehow negated. On the contrary, we are always in the middle of things – always in the midst of life and in the middle of language.[3] We are never going actually to encounter the great big terrifying nothingness that is supposed to encircle our life and negate all our values, so why should we allow ourselves to be troubled in any way by the thought of it?

A moral from all this is that we should be wary of the apologetic strategy, used quite commonly today, that invokes the spectre of nihilism in order to frighten us into accepting neo-dogmatism. The strategy works by playing a kind of Carrollian trick with the word 'nothing'. A phrase like 'You have nothing to be afraid of' may say 'Fear not', but it somehow cannot help also conveying the contrary impression, that nothing is perhaps something of which we should be very afraid indeed.[4] Wittgenstein's positivism about ordinary language and the life-world aims to stop that sort of illusion from developing and I have myself used the notion of outsidelessness to the same effect. Sometimes, I snap aggressively, 'Nothingness does not exist!' Got that? There's no such thing as nothing and the only cure for the fear of it is by learning to wait upon and to love life's sheer contingency and transience.

In summary, *transient ourselves, we should commit ourselves unreservedly to our own transient lives*, confident that there is not anything that threatens to rob us of either the meanings of the words we use or the values by which we live. Nor do we ever step outside life. We are always in the midst of life. We should be easy, going. We should have faith in life. Wherever we are is always the top of the world.

17

Expressionism

In much of traditional spirituality the way to find oneself and to become one's true self is by solitary recollection and introspection. One gathers oneself together and one turns inwards for self-examination. The real self is what St Paul calls 'the inner man';[1] the old appearance/reality distinction, when applied to the human person, suggests that the dressed-up, publicly presented outer self is only appearance and that the real self is the naked, hidden, interior, private self that is hidden behind the outer appearance. In Christian spirituality it is this interior self that endures and it is this interior self that relates itself to God.

However, I have been suggesting that in the second half of the twentieth century we abandoned the traditional belief in the superior reality of things hidden and inward, and instead began to see the self as becoming itself extravertively. Its natural movement is outwards, into symbolic expression. And it is through that movement outwards into expression that, briefly, we are able to get ourselves together and become ourselves.

On this account the outer and socially presented self is not a false mask, but the inner self's natural expression, as the latent becomes patent. But it is only a transient expression. We become ourselves and recognize ourselves en passant, as we pass out into language and pass away. Interestingly, the self is never something permanently achieved; we are able to become ourselves only in our passing out and away. We live by dying, becoming ourselves as we lose ourselves.

Where have we heard a story a little like this before? Perhaps in the speculative systems of early Iran and India or amongst the platonists and the gnostics of east Mediterranean antiquity or amongst the great German Idealists. Or perhaps in one or another of the heterodox speculative thinkers who crop up in all periods. These people love to unfold a huge circling myth of cosmic history. The story often begins with the Absolute or the world-ground in a remote, slumbering and undifferentiated condition. It is so abstract as to be unthinking and unthinkable. Then gradually, as it differentiates itself, it comes forward and out into clearer definition and expression. It becomes internally complex. Some disharmony or conflict appears within it, beginning a long struggle for reconciliation. Through that struggle the Absolute gradually becomes conscious of itself as it slowly returns into a clearer, higher-level and more achieved version of the primal unity. And that's what the whole of cosmic history is about: the Absolute most fully becomes itself by going out into multiplicity and then returning into unity. It casts a great shadow in order to see its own shape. The speculative thinker has to see cosmic history as moving in a circle, but also as making some kind of gain through that circular movement. The plot circles, but also spirals, so that it returns into itself at a higher level. So what's the gain? It has to be a gain in consciousness – as if the Absolute, *the Absolute*, has passed from innocence to experience! History as the *Bildungsroman* of God.

The average westerner is most likely to have met a version of this story in Valentinian Gnosticism or Kabbalistic Judaism or – more respectably – in Erigena or Hegel or indeed Jung. It is the biggest story of all, the ultimate grand narrative, and it is clearly a story that functions on two levels, for it tells of the first emergence of consciousness and its development towards a final state of comprehensive inclusion and reconciliation, a story which is the key story both of the whole of things and of each individual's life, so that if as I meditate upon the story I can feel that this is both the story of my own life and the story of everything, then I can find myself being taken up into the story and being made a part of the whole. And that is redemption.

The reason why I have introduced the big story here is that it has influenced many religious doctrine-systems, and most notably Christian theology. Over the years I have repeatedly found that things said about God in Christian theology are in fact coded presentations of ideas about the human self and its religious development. Here, the crucial idea is that spirit does not have any original reflexive knowledge of itself. To become self-conscious it must go out of itself into an Other, which is also itself and in which it can see itself. That is true for all of us and it is true even for God. Thus from all eternity, we gather, God in order to be himself has needed to go out of himself into expression in his own eternal Word or Son. Then God's gain in consciousness and his joy, as he recognizes and identifies with himself in his own expressed Word, is his own eternal Spirit, the Spirit that unites the Father and the Son. So in eternity the self can be most completely itself by eternally both going out into expression and also returning to reaffirm its own unity in the Spirit.

For us who live in time things are bound to be somewhat different, because temporal life is a continual passing away. We do not get our self-expression back again; we have to be content to let it go. But in Christian mythology God is pictured as having himself entered into this living-by-dying of ours, as his own expressed image enters time, takes human form and dies on the cross.

The death of God in Christ on the cross can thus be seen as a very grand mythical representation of the living-by-dying that all of us must undergo who seek to become selves in time. We can be happy, perhaps in love, perhaps in having children, and perhaps in creative work, but this achieved self-expression is continually slipping away from us. We have to let it pass. We never get to possess it personally and permanently. The Trinity symbolizes a state of perfect self-expression and self-possession that we can never realize in our finite and timebound selves – but it may successfully persuade us to seek such happiness by self-expression as is open to us. It may even persuade us that our continual self-loss is ethically necessary and a good thing.

I need now to explain a little further why we so much need to express ourselves. In mainline orthodox platonism the greatest need of the self is for purification, for self-mastery under the monarchical rule of reason and for contemplative knowledge, in the light of which we will know how to live rightly. But the doctrine to which I am drawing attention is one that has almost never been taught by a canonical philosopher: it is the doctrine that the self's first and greatest need is not the need for knowledge, but the need for expression. We need continually to become ourselves by expressing ourselves in symbols through which we can identify ourselves and give ourselves to others. In seeking to do this we are of course guided by a variety of role models: parents, peers, heroes and saints. And the very use of the term role model implies that in recent years we have come to see that the self is theatrical; it is a role that we enact, a part we play.

As a role that we enact, the self is in two senses a compromise. First it is a social compromise, in the sense that we have to work out terms on which we can fit into the social scene and find a niche that we can occupy. Second, the self like other works of art is a compromise in the sense that it has to synthesize, or symbolically to unify, a number of conflicting forces that compete furiously for expression. Those powerful conflicting forces within us cannot be reconciled in themselves; they can only be unified in and through our always-slightly-ambivalent symbolic expression. And that is why we are continually saying goodbye to the selves we are trying to become.

I have called this 'post-sainthood',[2] but it might be better to admit that this view of the self as an inevitably imperfect compromise and, in being in any case only a transient fiction, falls some way short of what is demanded by traditional ideas of holiness. Jesus tells us to be perfect as God is perfect,[3] but in saying that, he asks far too much of us. Our situation is a lot tougher than God's; we have to cope with living in time, with internally quarrelsome selves, with other people and with it all. Some sort of compromise and some sort of self we will all produce, because we must. If we live by a professional code or if we follow a good role model, we can do a bit better; if we live by the religious imagination we may do better still. But nobody's perfect and nobody can be perfect. Selfhood, like politics, is the art of the possible. At least one can try to put on a good show.

So far I have discussed our symbolic expression as the means
by which we produce our transient selves, the characters that we
play. But our symbolic expression is so rich and complex that it
is at the same time also world-building.

The self is constructed on the inner face of language and the
world is constructed on the outer face of language. On its inner
face, our utterance acts as a channel of expression for our always
mixed feelings; it makes them public in symbolic form, symbols
having the power to attract and discharge several strands of
feeling at once. And on its outer face, our utterance comes out
into public space and interacts with the utterance of others. Out
of this continual interaction there slowly develops the great
public consensus, the collection of customs, that we call our
world. Kant's philosophy still provides a good way in to the
point I'm trying to make: that our world of experience is a
human interpretation, all the way down:

Look at your visual field. Carry out a Kant-type transcendental analysis of what's in front of you. Ask how it is that you see
things, identifiable things, describable things with qualities, dis-
posed in space and persisting in time. You will find that everything that is given to you is already human: human the general
conceptual framework in which all things are set, human all the
categories through which they are thought, human the scientific
theory through which everything can be identified, understood
and described, human the feeling-responses that we call the
perceptual qualities, such as colour and taste and human all the
language in which alone you and I can say, think and check out
all of this. Our world is now a human world, all the way down.
We have gradually evolved amongst ourselves every bit of our
way of seeing, and therefore of what we see. Our world is our
own accumulated *oeuvre*, our self-objectification.[4]

Alternatively, here is a slightly different way in to the same
doctrine: over the past millennium and more, the French people
have evolved amongst themselves, in and through their processes
of symbolic exchange and co-operative work, the whole of the
great and complex geographical and cultural entity that we call
France. We no longer see anything as divinely instituted and just

given; we see everything as having been historically evolved within our corporate conversation.

What follows for religion from the expressionist view of the self and the world? We should now give up all ideas of withdrawing from the world in order to purify our souls in preparation for a better life after death. Instead, we should commit ourselves whole-heartedly to life. We should be content, by passing out into symbolic expression, to get ourselves together as best we can, to make our contribution to our world as well as we can and to put on a good show. If we love our world we'll be content to pass out into it, because we will see in it our objective redemption.

In summary, *we should pursue salvation, not by an ascetical withdrawal from the world, but by expressive living.* As we pour out into symbolic expression, we briefly get ourselves together and become ourselves and, more lastingly, we make our contribution to the common world as we pass out into it.

18

The union of life and death

In love, Juliet says to Romeo:

> My bounty is as boundless as the sea,
> My love as deep: the more I give to thee,
> The more I have, for both are infinite.[1]

'The more I give to thee, the more I have.' Juliet is saying that
there are certain qualities, certain things that exist only as we let
go of them or give them away. Indeed, the more generously we
give them away, the more they are multiplied. Mean people will
always be short of supplies, whereas generous and hospitable
people, like the widow of Zarephath who fed Elijah, can be
assured that their jar of meal and their cruse of oil will never be
empty.[2]

Juliet mentions bounty and love and we might add the
examples of selfhood and even life itself. These goods are like hot
potatoes: we can't cling to them, we have to let them go. And if
we have enough faith or trust in life to be generous in expending
them or letting them go, we will find that they are continuously
renewed.

A general point about personal and ethical life in time is being
made here – that from moment to moment we must venture
ourselves, hazard ourselves and cast our bread upon the waters.
Sometimes the rule is expressed in the form 'Freely you have
received; freely give,'[3] but experience seems rather to teach the
converse: if you give freely, you will receive freely.[4] We can live
easily only on the basis of a trust in life that requires us all the
time to let go and to risk ourselves. The more generously we are
able to do this, the more sure we can be that we will be re-

plenished. And indeed, in our very best periods we may find that wholehearted self-giving in love or work has the effect of filling us with an unequalled sense of vitality and exhilaration.

Everything here depends upon having the courage to jump. Faced with life's sheer contingency and the possibility – even the seeming probability – of disastrous loss or humiliating rejection, our first inclination may be towards hesitation, dithering, anxiety and (ultimately) despair. Where does one find the courage to risk everything? At this point, the Swiss Catholic theologian Hans Küng invokes what he calls a 'fundamental trust',[5] and wishes to interpret as an implicit faith in God; but he does not and cannot produce any very convincing argument for such an interpretation. When we dither in the face of the abyssal contingency and uncertainty of human life in time, we do not need to look for help to an old metaphysical idea of necessary and eternal Being. It's simply not relevant. What we really need is a personal habit of attending to and becoming easy and familiar with the purely contingent kind of Be-ing in and by which we do in fact have to live.

I accept the existentialist idea that our existence as finite and conscious beings who must live and act in time is often terrifying to us, because it involves something like a little death in every moment. To be, we must venture out upon, and float upon, pure contingency. How are we going to find the courage to do that and to love life? Not by attending to the absolute and self-existent being of the old metaphysical theism, but by attending to Be-ing – its finitude and contingency, its continuous gentle forthcoming in time – and so gradually learning the art of trusting Be-ing. Like Buddhists, we need to meditate upon the metaphysical emptiness of the passing show of existence, learn to live with it and even to venture forth upon it.

Gradually, we free ourselves of the mistaken idea that we are solid and substantial beings and that Be-ing will turn out to be too unbearably light to support us. On the contrary, we are exactly as light and transient as Be-ing itself is and as everything else is. So Be-ing is just right for us.

The philosophical shift needed in order to appreciate the point here is one that arrived in the West only very late, in the early nineteenth century. At that time, reason was enhistorized; that is, philosophical thinking began to come down into historical time and change and into the temporal flow of an ordinary human life. Previous philosophy had for the most part fixed its gaze upon the traditional order of reason: the world of necessary and *a priori* truth. Now, in writers like Kierkegaard, philosophy comes down into the point of view of the ordinary mortal who lives in time and must find the courage to act, to seek the truth and to become him/herself. Traditional rationalist philosophy was not primarily about the empirical world and human action, but about Plato's noumenal world, the world of eternal essences and *a priori* truths of reason. As such, it was not of much practical help to the ordinary person. What he/she needs is to meditate upon contingency, finitude and temporality; the slipping-away of everything in time of which he/she is a part. He/she needs to look at Buddhism and perhaps to revise his/her ideas about the religious object. That means dispensing with the traditional very absolutist idea of God and instead keeping company with the temporal outflow of Be-ing, which turns out to be a more congenial companion. Like the east Asian sage, one develops a taste for everything that is lightweight and transient: shadows, flames, bubbles, leaves, water, insects, clouds and everything that passes. One thinks: Everything is thus and so, and so am I.

This meditation on Be-ing and universal transience leads us to revise the traditional ideas about life and death as polar opposites and to see them instead as always intertwined in our experience.

Traditional theology was characterized by a strongly supernaturalist understanding of life. God was the living God, your life; Christ was the Way, the Truth and the Life, and the Resurrection and the Life; and the Holy Spirit was the Lord and Giver of Life.[6] In the traditional philosophical theology life as an attribute of God meant almighty causal power to jolt everything else into life. God was unmixed, pure life, like an infinite electric charge; death was a wretched state of darkness, isolation and impotence, cosmically at the furthest remove from God.

In modern thought, obviously much influenced by the turn of philosophy towards the human life-world and by modern biology, our life is our participation in the general going-on of things in the human life-world. Like Be-ing generally it is contingent, finite and temporal, like Be-ing it continually pours out, passes away and is replenished. It is very much what in Christian thought was called a dying life, and when we most wholeheartedly affirm it just as such, we call it eternal life.

This new and non-platonic sense of 'eternal' comes in during the early nineteenth century, but has a long previous history in religious art, where it is often symbolized by a fire, the sun or a fountain. In some cases where these symbols are used there could be a veiled allusion to Aristotle, who has a famous phrase[7] ('active stillness', perhaps?) suggesting a motion so even and continuous that it looks like a state of rest. A spinning top can appear still. In the same way, the fire, the sun and the fountain may seem to synthesize life and death, for they both pour out and pass away all the time and yet are evenly and continuously renewed all the time. The process by which they live is the same as the process by which they die. From a distance, they may seem still.

These images of fire, the sun and the fountain fascinate us because they suggest that death and life are not polar opposites, but are intertwined aspects of a single package. To live is in a certain sense to be dying all the time and to be on familiar terms with death. It is a commonplace observation that every living creature has some awareness of death. Nowhere is there pure life, without any admixture of dying. How could there possibly be personal life that is not transient? So we speak of eternal life when we accept the package and say a full Yes to this mortal life of ours. It is all there is; we are always in the midst of it, because there is no place outside it. The gospel idea that the believer has in a sense 'died already'[8] may be taken to mean that, in order to find the courage to live we must already have confronted death. To let go of traditional but illusory consolations and to have faced our life's pure contingency from moment to moment, is already to know the worst. And to be

able to say Yes to life and live it to the full is already to have con-
quered death.

In his usual rather bilious style, Arthur Schopenhauer declares
that:

> . . . undoubtedly it is the knowledge of death, and therewith
> the consideration of the suffering and misery of life, that give
> the strongest impulse to philosophical reflection and meta-
> physical explanations of the world . . . Although (religious)
> systems seem to make the existence of their gods the main
> point . . . this is only because they have tied up their teaching
> on immortality therewith . . . if we could guarantee their
> dogma of immortality to them in some other way, the lively
> ardour for their gods would at once cool.[9]

Well, I accept Schopenhauer's challenge. The hardest test for a
body of religious teaching such as is offered here is whether,
when we take it all in and change our attitudes and practices
accordingly, we do find ourselves liberated from the fear of
death. And I answer, Yes, it does work. Go short-termist, practise solar living, love life in its very transience and you will verify
the teaching.

In short, *life and death are not polar opposites and neither is
ever experienced 'pure'*. The two are always mingled, for life in
time always involves risk and the awareness of death. To be able
nevertheless to say Yes to life and live it to the full is already to
have eternal life.

19

Humanitarian ethics

O sola beatitudo! O beata solitudo! (Oh solitary blessedness! Oh blessed solitude!) Many of the ancient world religions originated in periods of political instability, psychological disturbance and deep 'world-pessimism'. They held that the devout person should seek perfection, but found that perfection cannot be pursued successfully while one lives in the world and is fettered by human ties. They concluded that one who seeks perfection must flee into the wilderness, far from human habitation, and there live a solitary ascetical life – whether for a preparatory period in one's life or during one's later years or perhaps for one's entire adult life.

In Christianity there were various sorts and degrees of solitariness. *Anchorites* and *anchoresses* (from *anachoreo*, to withdraw) might be walled up within a church, like Julian of Norwich. *Hermits* (from *eremia*, desert) were desert solitaries, *Coenobites* (from *koinos bios*, common life) were solitaries whose separate little houses were clustered together in a common enclosure. Each monk might be idiorrythmic (following his own rule, as in some monasteries on Mount Athos) or they might live under a common rule, as western monks do, with very varying rules about silence. The Carthusian house at Mount Grace in North Yorkshire still gives an excellent idea of their way of life.

Running through all this variety is a single thread: a very strong belief that the soul is an individual substance – that is, that the self is free-standing. It is distracted by company and flourishes in isolation. In solitude the self recollects itself and turns in upon itself. As its self-awareness becomes heightened and more clear, the relation to God comes to the fore and the self

becomes aware of its own sinfulness before God. But God knows
our sins and our needs better than any fellow human can and our
turning to him is quickly met by his therapeutic forgiveness.

Belief in the free-standing individual self and in the therapeutic
and religious efficacy of solitude remained very strong in the
West until the nineteenth century. In North America prisons
were called 'penitentiaries', a term drawn from Roman Catholicism, and prison cells were very like monk's cells. Solitude was
enforced both architecturally and by dress in a most striking
manner in many English prisons, as can still be seen in the chapel
at Lincoln Gaol, within the Castle.

It didn't work. The effect of enforced social isolation was not
to redeem prisoners but to drive them insane; in retrospect it is
extraordinary that Christianity – ostensibly the most humanistic
of religions, in which we are instructed that we are 'members one
of another'[1] – should for most of its history have been dominated
by extreme spiritual individualism in its metaphysics and by a
moral outlook that saw the company of other people as weakening and dissipating the self.

That metaphysics has now – but only now, that is, very recently – come to look weirdly mistaken. It was thought that a
human being came in two bits, body and soul, or body and mind;
but what was this thing, the mind or soul, that was 'in' the body
and somehow tied to it for the present, but which on the day of
our death would separate from the body and begin a new and
independent life in another world? How are we to describe the
doings, the various non-physical operations of 'the mind', such
as remembering, conjecturing, inferring and deciding? I am
bewildered by these questions, and haven't a clue how to
describe the 'mental' acts or operations of a non-physical entity
inside us.

The best guess I can offer, by way of explanation of these
strange ideas, is that spirits came first and rational souls were
thought as entities somewhat like spirits. A spirit was a very busy
but invisible intelligent agent, thought of as responsible for a
range of untoward events in our neighbourhood. People thought
they knew what a spirit was, and identified it through its opera-

tions. Further, spirits were perceived to be capable of entering persons and influencing their behaviour. It must therefore have seemed entirely reasonable to think of the soul or mind as being rather like an owner-occupier spirit, permanently resident in the body. It controls the body, governing its behaviour, but is also capable like a spirit of autonomously 'mental' operations such as being aware of itself.

My suggestion is, then, that it is because the mind or soul was thought of as being rather like a resident spirit that in our tradition there has been so strong a belief that we have inside us a free-standing autonomous being, an agent that is self-aware and performs a whole range of non-physical intellectual operations; a being that has its own hotline to God, within one's head. (Think how strange it is that in our tradition people have been so sure that independently, just inside their heads, they can contact the eternal world.)

As a result, our tradition was anti-humanitarian. The self was more-or-less complete on its own. It was a substance. It didn't really need society and it didn't need language in order to be itself. It did better in solitude with God.

Today, however, we think entirely differently and serious hermiting is scarcely imaginable. The thinking self, 'the mind', as I have been suggesting all along, is not something primary and free-standing, but more of a secondary effect. Self-consciousness, for example, is not something pure, founding and primary, but an internalized version of thinking about how we look in the eyes of others or in a mirror. Thinking itself is not primary and pre-linguistic, but internalized speech. (Who was it who said: 'How do I know what I think, until I hear what I say?') Mental arithmetic is not the natural ability of a pure rational spirit, but an imaginary refinement of our normal practice of working it out with the help of our fingers, a pencil, an abacus, the times tables, a ready reckoner, log-tables, a slide rule, a calculator or a computer. If we really are pure rational souls whose natural home is in the intelligible world, why on Earth are we so heavily dependent upon all those external promptings and aids to thought, such as aides-memoires, souvenirs, mementos, journals, shopping lists, diaries and knots in handkerchiefs? We are not naturally rational beings. For at least ninety-five per cent of humanity, ninety-five per cent of the time it is our public and objective social institutions that in various ways teach, persuade and sometimes compel us to behave more-or-less rationally. Isn't that obvious?

So there has been in modern times a gradual shift towards a more humanistic world-view and a humanitarian ethics, as we have slowly come to understand how completely we are embedded in history, in our social relations and in the to-and-fro of language.

Here is an illustration of how our thinking has changed. In the nineteenth-century debates about special creation versus evolution, it was famously asked whether in creating everything God had made Adam with a navel, trees with tree-rings inside their trunks and rocks with fossils embedded in them. Surely, it was suggested, God would have had to create a world with all the evidence of a past? But this enquiry is even more relevant to the question of the self. Could God have created Adam *ex nihilo*, as an adult with no memory, no formed emotional make-up, no age, no life-history, and would such an Adam, with no historically formed adult personality, be able to function as a human being? No, he would not. He'd have no self, no habits of expression. He wouldn't know who he was. He'd be a zombie, a bewildered cipher.[2] We human beings are completely embedded in language and in the section of the human world's history of which we are products. You are the outcome of your own life-history, which is the history of your communicative relations with others.

People used to claim that the old view of the self affirmed human dignity, and the idea is worth pursuing. The old western view of the cosmos as a great chain of being gave 'Man' a central position, on the hinge between the invisible creation and the visible creation. The human soul occupied the bottom rung of the ladder of things invisible. Above it were the nine orders of the angelic hierarchy. The human body, just one rung down from its soul, occupied the top position amongst things visible. Man was what in the army is called a Warrant Officer Class One, or perhaps a Quartermaster. At the summit of the lower orders, he could be seen as eligible for eventual co-optation into the officer class of spirits in Heaven. In short, although 'Man' was only one cog in a very large cosmic machine, he had reason to feel a certain modest pride. Everything hinged around him and the story of his fall and redemption was central to the main storyline of cosmic history.

The new position of humanity differs as much from the old as liberal democracy differs from feudalism. The human self (or soul) is no longer a substance and no longer has a supernatural destiny. It is now woven into the human world about us and the human language that has called us into being and now sustains us. Nothing radically non-human or anti-human either threatens us or rivals us. What becomes of us is on the whole our own responsibility. We belong just where we are and only our own indolence and lack of imagination (or perhaps, lack of freedom and opportunity) prevent us from making our lives very much better than they are. Certainly, we have no reason any longer for any cosmic feeling of injustice or dissatisfaction. On the contrary, we have come to a time of religious fulfilment. The appropriate ethical response is to identify ourselves completely with the passing show of things, saying Yes to life (solar ethics) and to commit ourselves to the utterly beliefless service of our fellow humans (humanitarian ethics).

Humanitarianism begins with the rise of the novel to be the dominant literary form, with the anti-slavery movement and with the founding of the Red Cross in Switzerland in 1863. Humanitarianism begins when disciplined anonymous professionals replace the earlier benefactors of the poor. Humanitarian aid is administered by people who do not represent any national, religious or ideological interest whatever and do not make any form of distinction between the 'deserving' and the 'undeserving'. Humanitarian ethics begins when the word 'humanitarian' has ceased to be a dirty word. In short, humanitarian ethics may be thought of as having begun at almost any time between the 1780s and the 1970s; the phrase indicates what has happened to morality in an age when there is no longer any sort of extra-human moral order. We take a pride in the fact that ethics is now founded just on our interwoven co-humanity and upon nothing else.[3]

People think that humanism and humanitarian ethics are some-how non-religious. They should take a look at any mediaeval representation of the heavenly world, eastern or western. It consists of almost nothing but an orderly crowd of very similar and equal human beings. Religion has long seen its ideal world as a radical-humanist world.

The point may be made in even stronger terms. On the walls of the Sistine Chapel in the Vatican, Michelangelo has represented the whole cycle of Christian doctrine, from Creation to the Last Judgment, simply in terms of the human body. That's radical humanism; think how unimaginable it is that a Muslim artist should ever do anything like it.

In summary, as we have already seen in chapter 15, religious meaning and value are now scatted across the whole of the life-world and as we have appropriated and differentiated the world we have spread something of ourselves across the whole life-world (see chapters 10 and 13). *The last stage in the historical evolution of religion is therefore universal religious humanism and the last ethic is humanitarian.*

20

My story, our story

When amongst people in general thinking at last becomes completely naturalistic, then people no longer look to any further world beyond this present world for their final happiness. Instead, we come to see ourselves as already living in the world at the end of the world, the last world, in which case we no longer need any great communal myth to keep us marching in step together towards the promised land. We are already at, or at least very close to, our final destination and we no longer expect conditions in general ever to become radically different from what they are now. We no longer believe in either progress or the communist society or life after death as a future destination, because we have already reached the end of the line. Such as it is, this is it, and the age of grand narratives of final redemption at the end of time is over. They have done their job and humankind's Long March is now coming to a halt.

However, there are a number of contrary considerations. The first is that individuals at least continue to live by stories.[1] Language as it runs always tells some kind of story and the way our physiology works helps to ensure that we continue to function in stories. In daily life, especially when we are joining a group and trying to pick up the thread of what's going on, we constantly work by framing and trying-out narrative hypotheses. In addition, everyone lives by some sort of personal life-story about where he/she is coming from and where he/she is trying to get to.

Meaningful personal life in time is bound to be storylike, and story-guided. Certainly stories will continue to play a large part in the lives of individual persons. But in addition, groups con-

`162`   *Philosophy's Own Religion*

tinue to define themselves in terms of stories about where they have come from and 'mission statements' about what they are hoping to achieve. The age of large-scale grand narratives of redemption at the end of time may be over, but for any human group to cohere there must be at the very least some harmonization of individual stories and some common goals.

I raise these general points by way of introduction to the question of whether there still needs to be any kind of church, in the sense of a distinct and organized religious society whose members have sacred stories, religious values and a good deal of vocabulary in common. The answer I am suggesting is that although old-style creeds and histories of salvation are now out of date, we do as much as ever need stories that will explain our present religious situation, telling us who we are by telling us where we've come from and how we got here.

This is a big subject – perhaps the biggest of all. During the fifteenth century the old religion-based civilizations began to decay and the modern age began. Since the seventeenth century,[2] we have been wondering anxiously about what has happened and what is becoming of us. How are we to interpret our present condition? Curiously – and perhaps inevitably – our attempts to describe what has happened tend still to be couched in the very vocabulary that we have rejected. After the end of the Middle Ages, the decline of Christendom and the Death of God, we may see ourselves as accursed fugitives and wanderers, like Cain. Or we may see ourselves as being like Milton's Adam and Eve, who have sinned and must leave Paradise on their long journey through history, while remaining under the protection of the very God against whom they have sinned. Trying to overcome these pessimistic interpretations, I have proposed a more Quakerish or 'American' theory, to the effect that we have come out of the oppressive disciplinary centuries of church history into a new post-historical era of religious freedom and fulfilment, for which kingdom-theology is going to be more appropriate. The great relative advantage of the USA at the turn of a new millennium is that unlike the old world it is not held back by disabling guilt or nostalgia for the lost sacred world of the Middle Ages.

I recognize that my argument in recent years may be seen as very 'New Labour' and as urging others in the old world to move over to something more like the American philosophy of religious history. We should not worry, I claim, about the decay of the church and the passing of the old disciplinary kind of religion. On the contrary, we should see these events as emancipatory, because they open up new possibilities of religious freedom and innovation. The kingdom-theology period promises to be longer, greater and more spacious than the ecclesiastical-theology period that we now see has ended.

So maybe we are like Cain, branded, the murderers of God. Maybe we are like Adam and Eve, exiled from Paradise to wander through history. Or maybe we are like early arrivals in America, fugitives from Christendom who rejoice that it is now possible to build the new world here on Earth. Or perhaps we are people who have come to the end of all the ideologies, religious and political. We are nihilists, wondering what to do with ourselves and what to make of ourselves. Some claim that our only recourse is to accept divine revelation and return to traditional religion.

I conclude that *we no longer require any great narrative scheme of doctrine: the old systematic theology should be replaced by storytelling about the religious significance of our own time and the history that has brought us to it.* No great authoritative and catholic church is required any more, thank God, and its place should be taken by informal religious associations like the Society of Friends, through which individuals may be helped to develop religious skills such as meditation, a religious vocabulary and their own personal life-stories.

21

Local colour

Describing her visit to Lhasa in August 1998, an Emmanuel College undergraduate wrote that 'It became increasingly evident that to come to Tibet as a tourist is to assist in China's plan to render Tibetans cultural relics in their own country.'[1]

What is happening in Lhasa is a vivid and extreme example of a process currently taking place all over the world, as the principal surviving monuments of the old pre-modern culture are engulfed by the heritage industry for conversion into tourist attractions, a process which with extraordinary completeness both preserves and destroys them. It is politically very convenient to the Chinese that they can simultaneously 'conserve' Tibetan culture and obliterate it, while at the same time turning it into a very useful generator of revenue from tourism.

The heritagization of Tibet is forced, but in the West the same process, equally lethal, is carried out voluntarily. Often there is a curious timeshare arrangement whereby for a time or a season a building is briefly restored to its traditional use, before reverting to its normal state of embalmed heritagization. This schizoid state of affairs suits the British very well and can be observed in our cathedrals, stately homes and royal palaces. In the Oxford and Cambridge colleges we have been obliged to learn the art of functioning simultaneously as working institution and as mythical, mummified tourist attraction. Some scientists find all the playacting a little distasteful and prefer to steer clear of college life; other people may become so caught up by the myth that they begin to act, and even to dress, like characters from *Zuleika Dobson* and *Decline and Fall*. But this is not the place to tell tales.

In all its forms, the process of heritagization bears eloquent witness both to our nostalgia for tradition and to its utter and total destruction. We are forced to realize that our own tradition is no longer ours: we can look at it only as a dead specimen, under glass. The world as it was – its customs, its values, its beliefs – is gone beyond recall. It is odd to reflect that the mass of people would never have voted for such comprehensive destruction. Most of them deplore it, but it is happening unstoppably, nevertheless. It is almost complete.

In this whole process the greatest loss of all has occurred in the field of religion. Holy places, traditional places of pilgrimage, are both the prime candidates for heritagization and also the places most completely destroyed by it. To visit a former holy place now heritagized is like visiting a robbed and empty grave. And it is against this sobering background that we have to ask, at the end of this study, how much can be retained of all the various local customs and 'over-beliefs' that the great religions have added to the very broad and general outline that has been described? For I see that globalization and the accompanying collapse of tradition has brought us back in many ways to eighteenth-century questions and ways of thinking. I have sketched a future common world philosophy and religious outlook. It is a language-mediated radical religious humanism and it is a religion of life, this life, and I have situated it approximately where eighteenth-century writers used to put what they called natural theology and natural religion. The eighteenth-century writers went on to ask what we should think about the various supplements – institutions, doctrines, customs, rituals, religious law – that are added to the common core by the revealed theologies of the various 'positive religions'. Much of this material consisted of badges of difference, by which the great faith-traditions distinguished themselves from each other. It was usually (and still is) precisely the most non-rational bits of your religion that you picked out and clung to the most fiercely, because they made such effective tokens of your distinct identity. But in a globalized world, how much of all this local colour can hope to survive as living tradition?

I fear the answer is that much of it will be kept as dead heritage. Like the religion of Bali, it will long be profitable as a tourist attraction, but almost nothing of it will survive as living tradition.[2] The cultural rupture now occurring is too great. The 'cathedral' solution, whereby a fragment of supposedly living religion is preserved within a thoroughly heritagized setting, fails and fails badly. In Japan, Imperial and Shrine Shinto ceremonies are still performed in what seems to be the old way, and in all the old places, but how much real difference to the world and to people's lives does their performance make now? None at all, of course. When in some great temple or shrine religious rites are maintained as heritage, encapsulated, the persons who are going through the motions may congratulate themselves upon their own traditionalism and their orthodoxy, but in terms of their cultural significance they are on a par with those aristocrats who are permitted to continue in occupation of a small reserved corner of the great house after it has been turned into a tourist destination. They linger on as caretakers in what was once their own house. They have come down in the world so much that their continuing presence is now something of an embarrassment. Similarly, the oddly bland co-existence of religion with its own heritagization is embarrassing; it is even almost unclean. I have to say, it disgusts me.

The religious object

Until during the twentieth century when Buddhism at last became well understood in the West, it was generally assumed that there would always be a religious object in some form or another. In popular language, if not a personal God, then perhaps 'the absolute', the whole and if not that, then a power, 'something greater than ourselves' or perhaps a life-force or just the sacred. Religious feeling was thought to seek an object to which it can relate itself and if it is disappointed in one quarter it will look to another.

A few western philosophers, such as Thomas Hobbes, were known to have put forward a 'non-cognitive', 'non-realist' or purely expressive account of religious language. On Hobbes's view, people's talk about God does not describe anything, but simply expresses their own ignorance, dread and sacred awe. But Hobbes's non-realism was usually taken simply for 'atheism' and was not thought to represent a serious contribution to the philosophy of religion.

Today's better knowledge of Asian philosophy and of Buddhism in particular obliges us to ask whether in future religion needs to have an object at all. I reply that, in the first place, after the end of metaphysics, the religious object is not a substance and therefore not compulsorily One, in the old way. As we have seen, it has become de-centred and disseminated. It may be Be-ing, just gentle forthcoming contingency. It may be everything that is in being, the whole fountain, the concrete out-pouring of everything, And it may be 'brightness', the lighting-up, by language, in consciousness, of everything, for us. Bright-ness is, I now find, the most readily accessible and reliable source of religious joy. Get a painter like the late Patrick Heron to show you.

Alternatively, I should perhaps end by admitting that I have not been able to get completely clear about the relation between Being, language and the self. Our condition remains incomplete, mysterious and not fully resolved, in a way that unfixes all dogmatic views and makes us 'post-everything'. And this too is perhaps a religious state that we can learn to love.

In conclusion, *for the sake of our spiritual integrity, it is best for the present not to insist too much upon the merely local and 'positive' features of religion.* We can't be sure that anything of them will survive or deserves to survive. And *there is no great and unique religious object, but we can appropriately take up religious attitudes towards bare pre-linguistic Be-ing, towards the whole fountain of actual Being and towards the brightness of everything.*

Notes

Preface

1. Don Cupitt, The Last Philosophy, London: SCM Press 1995.
2. Don Cupitt, *The Meaning of It All in Everyday Speech*, London: SCM Press 1999, chapter 28, pp. 101ff. and Don Cupitt, *Kingdom Come in Everyday Speech*, London: SCM Press 2000, pp. 3f. The point being made here about ordinary language's own philosophy suggests a neat and brief way of describing the difference between John Milbank and me. Milbank thinks that philosophy by itself drives towards and ends in nihilism, from which we must escape, and do so by accepting divine Revelation; whereas I say that philosophy ends when it comes at last to ordinary language's own philosophy – which turns out to be very much what religion has called kingdom theology. So, after seven or so centuries of growing apart, philosophy and religion embrace each other again at the end of history.
3. Americans also say 'hit it up' and 'hit it with'.
4. The exhibition, 'Heaven', opened in 1999 at Dusseldorf and then at the Tate, Liverpool.
5. Trevor Beeson, *Rebels and Reformers: Christian Renewal in the Twentieth Century*, London: SCM Press 1999.

1. Dogmatic theology and the philosophy of religion

1. G. W. H. Lampe (ed.), *A Patristic Greek Lexicon*, Oxford: Clarendon Press 1961, s.v.
2. There is a useful short account of the history of 'theology' in Wolfhart Pannenburg, *Theology and the Philosophy of Science*, London: Darton, Longman and Todd 1976.
3. See Don Cupitt, *Mysticism After Modernity*, Oxford: Blackwell 1998.
4. Peter C. Hodgson (ed.), *G. W. F. Hegel: Lectures on the Philosophy of Religion. One-Volume Edition: The Lectures of 1827*, Berkeley: University of California Press 1988.
5. Joseph Butler, *The Analogy of Religion*, 1736, Introduction, paragraph 3.
6. Joseph Butler, *The Analogy of Religion*, advertisement.

7. Ernest Gellner, *Legitimation of Belief*, Cambridge: Cambridge University Press 1974, pp. 28f.

8. See Don Cupitt, *The New Religion of Life in Everyday Speech*, London: SCM Press 1999, p. 17.

9. Alexander Baumgarten, *Aesthetica*, 1750.

10. Slavoj Žižek, *The Plague of Fantasies*, London: Verso 1997, pp. 106ff.

2. Globalization and religious thought

1. See Vernon F. Storr, *Development and Divine Purpose*, London: Methuen 1906.

2. For the slowly developing syllabus, see *The Cambridge Students' Handbook*, 1919/20, pp. 500f.; 1963/64, pp. 398f.

3. Microscoft, *ENCARTA Dictionary of World English*, London: Bloomsbury 1999.

4. See chapter 1, note 4.

5. See E. Troeltsch, *The Absoluteness of Christianity and the History of Religions*, 1901.

6. Rudolf Otto, *Das Heilige* (trans. as *The Idea of the Holy*), 1917.

7. For example, W. T. Stace, *Mysticism and Philosophy*, London: Macmillan 1961.

8. For example, John Hick, *The Fifth Dimension*, Oxford: One World 1999.

9. See Dale S. Wright, *Philosophical Meditations on Zen Buddhism*, Cambridge: Cambridge University Press 1998.

10. A valiant attempt to break Buddhism out of its historical origins and cultural wrappings is Stephen Bachelor's *Buddhism Without Beliefs*, New York: Riverhead Books 1997. But is the outcome still Buddhism, and still a religion?

11. Several versions of this story are mentioned by Dale S. Wright, *Philosophical Meditations on Zen Buddhism*, for example pp. 92f.

12. Kierkegaard's chief discussion of this point occurs in the *Concluding Unscientific Postscript*, 1846; Swenson/Lowrie translation, Princeton University Press 1941, pp. 24ff.

13. Jacques Derrida and Gianni Vattimo (eds), *Religion*, Cambridge: Polity Press 1998, pp. 20ff. See also the classic work on this topic, Wilfred Cantwell Smith, *The Meaning and End of Religion*, New York: Macmillan 1962.

14. See Geoffrey Samuel, *Civilized Shamans: Buddhism in Tibetan societies*, Washington: The Smithsonian Institution 1993.

3. On systematic 'closure'

1. On all this, see the writings of Slavoj Žižek, for example, Slavoj Žižek/ F. W. J. Schelling, *The Abyss of Freedom/Ages of the World: An Essay by Slavoj Žižek with the text of Schelling's* Die Weltalter *(second draft, 1813) in English translation by Judith Norman*, Ann Arbor: the University of Michigan Press 1997.

2. Kurt Gödel, 'Über formale unentscheidbare Sätze der Principia Mathematica und verwandter Systeme', *Monatshefte für Mathematik und Physik*, 1931 – with a substantial secondary literature.

3. And I confess that I have always been attracted to systematicity, ever since the six weeks of manic excitement in the summer of 1973 during which I wrote *The Leap of Reason* (eventually published in 1976). Since then I have found on about nine or ten occasions that in the highest state of excitement I always go systematic, with a feeling of soaring speculative confidence. Is system manic?

4. This view was proposed in Don Cupitt, *The Last Philosophy*, London: SCM Press 1995. Perhaps I took it from Wittgenstein, who reportedly saw the great metaphysical systems of the past as being like large-scale and complex works of art. But, with typical perversity, he thought that we moderns ought to discipline ourselves not to think and write in those ways. Why? See, for example, Rush Rhees (ed.), *Ludwig Wittgenstein: personal recollections*, Oxford: Basil Blackwell 1981, p. 120.

5. Don Cupitt, *Solar Ethics*, London: SCM Press 1995, p. 56.

4. Beginning all over

1. See John 1.14, 17; 4.23; 5.33; 8.32, 40, 44, 45, 46; 14.6; 16.7, 13; 17.17, 19; 18.37, 38.

2. William James, *The Varieties of Religious Experience*, early editions, p.514: 'The religious question is primarily a question of life, of living or not living in the higher union which opens itself to us as a gift.'

3. A good, short and familiar text on which to try out a non-metaphysical reading of the Bible is I John 4.7–12. Is 'God is love' fully and straightforwardly convertible with 'Love is God'? Yes.

It is worth pointing out here that the dogmatic–realist misreading of the biblical text is taught by our vernacular translations. For example, in the original text there is no distinction between capital and lower-case letters. But in translation the distinction is introduced, and is used to cue a dogmatic–realist reading of words like Son and Spirit. This persuades readers that the New Testament writers see Christ as being the Son of God in a unique sense, peacemakers and suchlike being merely sons of God.

4. This point about 'theism' is much made by Nicholas Lash and some

other recent writers. See Lash's *Easter in Ordinary*, London: SCM Press 1988, pp. 103f.: 'As Christians, we can dispense with theism.'

5. Lewis Carroll, who uses this phrase in *Through the Looking Glass*, was a member of the clergy, and can scarcely have been unaware of its religious implications.

6. So far as the question still needs to be mentioned at all, I include supposed 'revealed truths' in this category.

5. How it is with us

1. Martin Heidegger, *Being and Time* (*Sein und Zeit*, 1927), trans. John Macquarrie and Edward Robinson, Oxford: Blackwell 1962.

6. The relation between language and reality

1. For Being, Man and Language, see my 1998 Being-books: Don Cupitt, *The Religion of Being*, London: SCM Press and Don Cupitt, *The Revelation of Being*, London: SCM Press.

2. Slavoj Žižek sees modern philosophy's shift away from necessity, eternity and perfection, and towards contingency, temporality and finitude as taking place in Schelling's weirdly original treatment of the Absolute. See chapter 3, note 1.

3. Nietzsche asks these questions more clearly and forcefully than anyone else. My answer to them is what I call 'solar ethics'.

4. Thanks to John Cupitt for help here.

5. Don Cupitt, *Creation Out of Nothing*, London: SCM Press and Philadelphia: Trinity Press International 1990, pp. 157ff.

7. 'Discursive idealism' and religious thought

1. Mircea Eliade, *Patterns in Comparative Religion*, London and New York: Sheed and Ward 1958, p. 410.

2. Ibid.

3. For what follows, see the text translated with notes in J. B. Pritchard (ed.), *Ancient Near Eastern Texts*, third edn with supplement, Princeton: Princeton University Press 1969, pp. 4f. I have very slightly simplified the appearance of the passages quoted.

4. Ibid., p. 5, column 2.

5. Psalms 19.1, RSV.

6. G. J. Warnock, *Berkeley*, London: Penguin Books 1953, p. 123.

7. From Schubert's *Die Winterreise* (1827), no. 22: 'Mut'. The lyric is by Wilhelm Müller.

8. All these points are made very well and in detail by Mark C. Taylor in his *About Religion*, Chicago: Chicago University Press 1999, for example on pp. 1–6. I have some pages about the transformations of the religious object in recent times in Don Cupitt, *The New Religion of Life in Everyday Speech*, London: SCM Press 1999, chapter 6.

8. The sign which denies that it is a sign

1. For example, 'Words and chess pieces are analogous: knowing how to use a word is like knowing how to move a chess piece.' From Alice Ambrose (ed.), *Wittgenstein's Lectures, Cambridge 1932–1935*, Oxford: Basil Blackwell 1979, p. 4. The same observation comes through into the *Philosophical Investigations* (1953), at no. 563ff.

2. Donald Hudson (W. D. Hudson), *Ludwig Wittgenstein: the bearing of his philosophy upon religious belief*, London: Lutterworth Press 1968, p. 63. Note the reference to T. R. Miles's phrase, 'the absolute existence mistake', from his book *Religion and the Scientific Outlook*, London: Allen and Unwin 1959.

3. Many striking and interesting sayings to this effect are reported in Rush Rhees (ed.), *Ludwig Wittgenstein: Personal Recollections*, Oxford: Basil Blackwell 1981 and in Ludwig Wittgenstein, *Culture and Value*, Oxford: Basil Blackwell 1980.

4. Think, for example, of the plays of Beckett and Ionesco.

5. The best introduction is still M. J. Charlesworth, *St Anselm's 'Proslogion' with 'A Reply on Behalf of the Fool' by Gaunilo and 'The Author's Reply to Gaunilo'*, Oxford: Clarendon Press 1965.

6. A useful symposium is John Hick and Arthur C. McGill, *The Many-Faced Argument*, New York: Macmillan 1967.

7. In what follows I am both indebted to and departing from Mark C. Taylor's discussions in his *About Religion* (see chapter 7, note 8). See also chapters 1 and 6.

8. Mark C. Taylor, *About Religion*, p. 165.

9. Being

1. In this chapter I am rethinking and slightly developing ideas first broached in Don Cupitt, *The Last Philosophy*, London: SCM Press 1995, Don Cupitt, *The Religion of Being*, London: SCM Press 1998 and Don Cupitt, *The Revelation of Being*, London: SCM Press 1998. I formed these ideas in dialogue with Heidegger, but they are here presented independently.

2. Berkeley nowhere uses exactly these words. The nearest he gets is in

Philosophical Commentaries 429: 'Existence is percipi or percipere, or velle i.e. agere'. But the formula as I quoted it fairly summarizes his doctrine.

3. Edward Craig, *The Mind of God and the Works of Man*, Cambridge: Cambridge University Press 1987, chapter 1 remains an excellent summary.

4. F. Nietzsche, *The Genealogy of Morals*, XXVII to the end.

5. See chapter 6.

6. Richard Rorty has been for twenty years the leading critic of representationalism. For a brief statement, see his 'Pragmatism as Anti-representationalism', the introduction to John P. Murphy, *Pragmatism: From Peirce to Davidson*, Boulder: Westview Press 1990. For a tough and combative statement of the opposite view, see Thomas Nagel, *The Last Word*, New York and Oxford: Oxford University Press 1997. One of the chief difficulties in Nagel's position concerns his supernaturalism of reason: if we ourselves came into being in the manner described by Darwin, how did we acquire such a world-transcending faculty?

7. Compare my argument here with Berkeley's oft-repeated assertion that his view of things, which at first seems so paradoxical, is no more than 'common sense'. Just like him, I'm claiming that when we discard an unnecessary, redundant layer of reality (his 'matter', my 'real world out there, which language copies') everything becomes brighter, fresher and more ours.

8. For more detail on this see Don Cupitt, *The Revelation of Being*, London: SCM Press 1998, chapter 2, note 1, pp. 107f.

9. This metaphor was broached in Don Cupitt, *After All*, London: SCM Press 1994, pp. 59f. and revised in Don Cupitt, *The Last Philosophy*, London: SCM Press 1995, pp. 64f.

10. *The web of communication*

1. The first recorded use of the phrase is late fifteenth century. In the sixteenth century the republic's citizens were chiefly 'Humanist' men of letters. But in retrospect its real importance lies in the part it played in the take-off of natural science between Galileo and the generation of Leibniz and Newton. See Peter Burke, 'Erasmus and the republic of letters', *European Review*, vol.7, no.1, pp. 5–17.

2. This term was introduced by Jean Baudrillard.

3. For the idea of the world as a communications-network, see Don Cupitt, *Only Human*, London: SCM Press 1985, pp. 192ff.

11. *We*

1. Genesis 1.3.

2. Evgeny Zamiatin, *We*, New York 1924, written in Russia in 1920.

3. So far as I know, nobody has ever written a philosophy of the public realm. Why not?

12. *I: the first person singular*

1. The term 'existentialism' was popularized by Sartre's very widely read *L'Existentialisme est un humanisme*, 1946; ET in *Existentialism and Humanism*, London: Methuen 1948. Typical 1950s introductions for English-speaking readers were published by F. C. Copleston and F. H. Heinemann (1953). Amongst recent books see George Pattison, *Anxious Angels: A retrospective view of religious existentialism*, London: Macmillan, and New York: St Martin's Press Inc. 1999.

2. The classic proof text for this was Philippians 2.12f.

3. See the famous journal entry headed 'Berlin, May 17, 1843'.

4. James Joyce, *Ulysses*, London: The Bodley Head 1960, pp. 871ff.

5. Brightening = intellectual 'illumination', or consciousness. It is also equivalent to Heidegger's term *Lichtung*.

13. *Our world*

1. See Don Cupitt, *Kingdom Come in Everyday Speech*, London: SCM Press 2000.

2. Ecdysis is the shedding of its outer skin, which a caterpillar may do six or eight times during its growth. The word metamorphosis is used for the greater change that occurs when, for example, the adult insect emerges from the pupa. I am suggesting that it is too late for gradualist reform; we need a major mutation.

3. The argument in these paragraphs is derived from my Everyday Speech series of short books (published by SCM Press 1999–2000), cited earlier.

4. The arguments that follow were first put forward in Don Cupitt, *After All*, London: SCM Press 1994.

14. *Reality and the imagination*

1. The way Berkeley treats the continuing existence of things between our perceptions of them leads him to emphasize, more strongly than most, God's continual sustaining of things in being by keeping them in mind.

2. Currently, Thomas Nagel, *The Last Word*, Oxford: Oxford University Press 1997 is the most eloquent defender of the old Enlightenment–rationalist conception of reason. For him and for philosophers like him, reason fits very neatly into the slot left vacant by the lost God.

3. See chapter10 and in particular note1. The first form of the appeal to
general consent as a touchstone of truth was the Vincentian Canon (*quod
ubique, quod semper, quod ad omnibus creditum est*: 'What has been
believed everywhere, always and by all'), laid down by Vincent of Lérins
(early fifth century).

15. Dissemination

1. The following are examples of books that show how intellectually
formidable Buddhism currently looks: *The Fundamental Wisdom of the
Middle Way: Nagarjuna's Mulamadhyamakakarika*, trans. and commen-
tary by Jay L. Garfield, New York and Oxford: Oxford University Press
1995; C. W. Huntingdon, Jr, *The Emptiness of Emptiness: an introduction
to early Indian Madhyamika*, Honolulu: University of Hawaii Press 1989;
Dale S. Wright, *Philosophical Meditations on Zen Buddhism*, Cambridge:
Cambridge University Press 1998; Joan Stambaugh, *Impermanence is
Buddha-Nature: Dogen's understanding of temporality*, Honolulu: University of Hawaii Press 1990.
2. See Don Cupitt, *Kingdom Come in Everyday Speech*, London: SCM
Press, 2000.
3. Georges Bataille treats death and immanence as equivalent. Notice
that the gods may die by going too far into transcendence, as they are
promoted into obscurity, like Chronos. They become unknowable and lose
interest in humans, as in Epicureanism. But, in the opposite direction, God
may also die by being returned into complete immanence within the human
realm, as happens in radical Christianity. This is the fulfilment of the idea of
God: God dies, not of irrelevance, but by giving himself unreservedly into
human beings.
4. 'There has been only one Christian, and he died on the Cross. The
'Evangel' died on the Cross. What was called 'Evangel' from this moment
onwards was already the opposite of what he had lived . . .', F. W.
Nietzsche, *The Anti-Christ*, 39.

16. Easy, going

1. Plato's *Republic*, 488 b-e.
2. Attributed to Keynes by Claude Cockburn and by A. C. Pigou.
3. 'Isn't it curious that although I know I have not long to live, I never
find myself thinking about a "future life". All my interest is still on this life
and the writing I am still able to do' – Wittgenstein in 1951, quoted by
M. O'C. Drury in Rush Rhees (ed.), *Ludwig Wittgenstein: personal recollections*, Oxford: Basil Blackwell 1981, p.183.
4. Lewis Caroll, *Through the Looking Glass*, VII, 'The Lion and the

Unicorn' discusses two examples: Alice's 'I see nobody on the road' and the Messenger's 'I'm sure nobody walks faster than I do'.

17. Expressionism

1. II Corinthians 4.16; Romans 7.22; Ephesians 3.16.
2. Don Cupitt, *After God*, London: Weidenfeld and Nicholson 1997, p. 90.
3. Matthew 5.48.
4. Don Cupitt, *The Last Philosophy*, London: SCM Press 1995, pp. 59f., slightly amended.

18. The union of life and death

1. William Shakespeare, *Romeo and Juliet* II, ii.
2. I Kings 16.8–16.
3. Matthew 10.8.
4. 'The measure you give will be the measure you get, and still more will be given you,' Mark 4.24; compare Matthew 7.2 and Luke 6.38.
5. Hans Küng, *Does God Exist? An Answer for Today*, London: Collins 1978.
6. I should have remarked in *The New Religion of Life in Everyday Speech* (Don Cupitt, London: SCM Press 1999) that stock phrases associate all three persons of the Trinity very closely with life. This close association has made much easier the recent sacralization of life.
7. Aristotle, *Energeia akinesias,* in *Nicomachean Ethics* VII, 14 (1154b27). 'If any being had a simple nature, the same activity would always give him the greatest pleasure. That is why God enjoys one simple pleasure for ever. For there is an activity not only of movement but also one of immobility . . .', from J. A. K. Thomson's translation, Harmondsworth: Penguin Books 1953, revised edition 1976, p. 257.
8. See for example John 5.24. I have avoided in this chapter repeating the ideas about solar living (expressionist spirituality) that I have set out elsewhere. For references, see Don Cupitt, *The Revelation of Being*, London: SCM Press 1998, chapter 9, note 3.
9. Arthur Schopenhauer, *The World as Will and Representation*, trans. E. F. J. Payne, New York: Dover Books 1966, Volume II, p. 161 (supplementary chapter XVII).

19. Humanitarian ethics

1. Romans 12.5.
2. The Golem and Frankenstein's monster were 'zombies, bewildered

ciphers'. So why has nobody remarked that Adam would have been so, too?

3. On these topics, see Don Cupitt, *Kingdom Come in Everyday Speech*, London: SCM Press 2000, chapters 7 and 9.

20. *My story, our story*

1. In this brief chapter I draw upon the account of stories given in Don Cupitt, *What is a Story?*, London: SCM Press 1990.

2. I suggest that John Milton's *Paradise Lost* (1667) can be read as reflecting anxiety that emergent modernity has involved a fresh Fall of Man.

21. *Local colour*

1. Sarah McMillan, in *The Emmanuel College Magazine*, Volume LXXXI, 1998–99, p. 72.

2. The reader will retort that much in my whole account is of specifically Christian origin. Yes it is, but I am careful not to label it too explicitly. I cling to it, because I think it to be of universal value and interest. I'd like to smuggle it through. The point I'm making here is neatly exemplified by the teaching of Jesus, which is already largely forgotten, even within Christianity. I quote and draw upon it a good deal, but I don't label it and I think we must accept that he is probably going to disappear. But I will still carry on with my smuggling.

Index